America by the Sea

EXPLORE AMERICA

America by the Sea

Reader's Digest

THE READER'S DIGEST ASSOCIATION, INC.
Pleasantville, New York / Montreal

AMERICA BY THE SEA was created and produced by **St. Remy Press**.

STAFF FOR AMERICA BY THE SEA
Series Editor: Elizabeth Cameron
Art Director: Solange Laberge
Editor: Alfred LeMaitre
Photo Researchers: Geneviève Monette
Cartography: Hélène Dion, Anne-Marie Lemay,
David Widgington
Researchers: Jennifer Meltzer, Robert B. Ronald
Contributing Researcher: Joan McKenna
Copy Editor: Judy Yelon
Index: Christine Jacobs
System Coordinator: Éric Beaulieu
Technical Support: Mathieu Raymond-Beaubien, Jean Sirois
Scanner Operators: Martin Francoeur, Sara Grynspan

ST. REMY STAFF
PUBLISHER: Kenneth Winchester
PRESIDENT, CHIEF EXECUTIVE OFFICER: Fernand Lecoq
PRESIDENT, CHIEF OPERATING OFFICER: Pierre Léveillé
VICE PRESIDENT, FINANCE: Natalie Watanabe
MANAGING EDITOR: Carolyn Jackson
MANAGING ART DIRECTOR: Diane Denoncourt
PRODUCTION MANAGER: Michelle Turbide

Writers: Rita Ariyoshi—Kauai
Michael Collier—Santa Catalina Island
Sharon Dan—St. John
Bob Devine—Monterey to Big Sur,
The Olympic Peninsula
David Dunbar—Cape Cod, Old San Juan
Jim Henderson—Galveston Island
M. Timothy O'Keefe—Biscayne National Park
James S. Wamsley—The Outer Banks

Contributing Writers: Adriana Barton,
Fiona Gilsenan, Elizabeth W. Lewis, Garet Markvoort, Enza Micheletti

READER'S DIGEST STAFF
Series Editor: Gayla Visali
Editor: Jill Maynard
Art Director: Evelyn Bauer
Art Editor: Nancy Mace

READER'S DIGEST GENERAL BOOKS
Editor-in-Chief, Books and Home Entertainment:
Barbara J. Morgan
Editor, U.S. General Books: Susan Wernert Lewis
Editorial Director: Jane Polley
Art Director: Evelyn Bauer
Research Director: Laurel A. Gilbride
Affinity Directors: Will Bradbury, Jim Dwyer, Joseph
Gonzalez, Kaari Ward
Design Directors: Perri DeFino, Robert M. Grant,
Joel Musler
Business Manager: Vidya Tejwani
Copy Chief: Edward W. Atkinson
Picture Editor: Marion Bodine
Head Librarian: Jo Manning

READER'S DIGEST PRODUCTION
Assistant Production Supervisor: Mike Gallo
Prepress Specialist: Karen Goldsmith
Quality Control Manager: Ann Kennedy Harris
Assistant Production Manager: Michael R. Kuzma

Book Production Director: Robert G. Whitton, Jr.
Prepress Manager: Garry Hansen
Book Production Manager: Patricia M. Heinz
U.S. Prepress Manager: Mark P. Merritt

The credits and acknowledgments that appear on page 144
are hereby made a part of this copyright page.

Copyright © 1996 The Reader's Digest Association, Inc.
Copyright © 1996 The Reader's Digest Association (Canada) Ltd.
Copyright © 1996 Reader's Digest Association Far East Ltd.
Philippine Copyright 1996 Reader's Digest Association Far East Ltd.

Library of Congress Cataloging in Publication Data

America by the Sea.
       p.   cm.—(Explore America)
    Includes index.
    ISBN 0-89577-864-5
    1. United States—Guidebooks. 2. Coasts—United States—
Guidebooks.   I. Reader's Digest Association.   II. Series.
E158.A47 1996
917.304'929—dc20   95-26793

Printed in the United States of America

Opening photographs
Cover: Monterey Coast, California
Back Cover: Sea otter, Alaska
Page 2: Rialto Beach, Olympic National Park, Washington
Page 5: Cape Neddick Light, Kennebunkport, Maine

CONTENTS

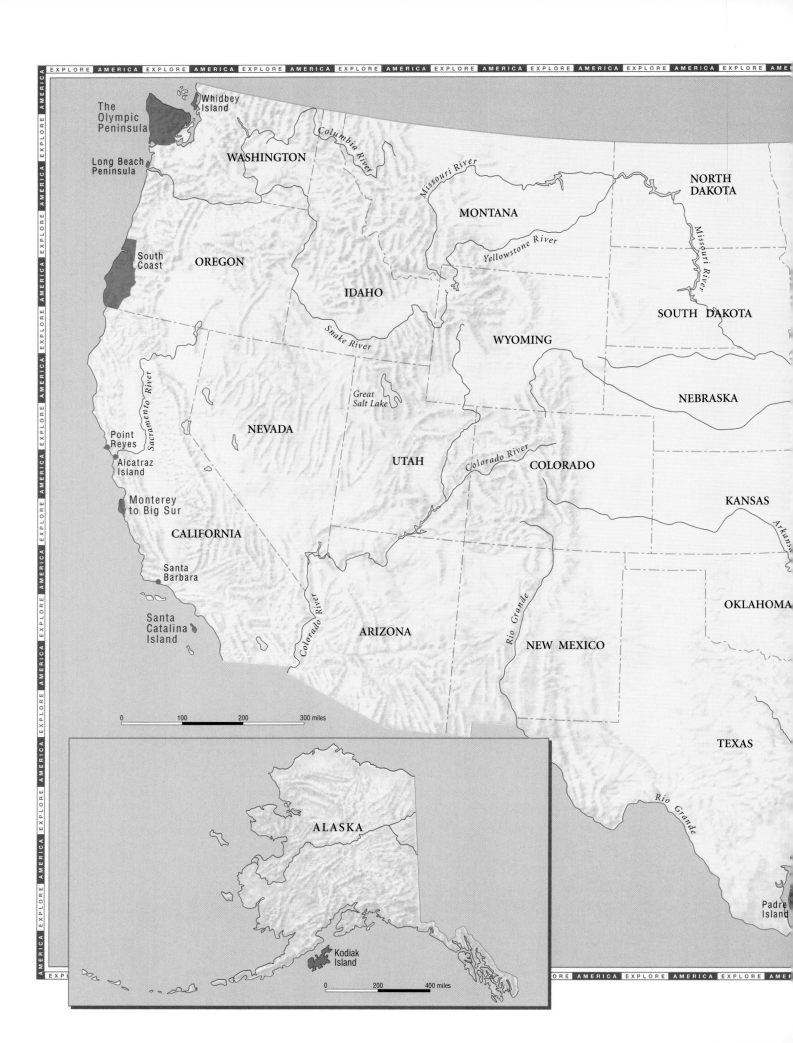

The
Olympic
Peninsula

Whidbey
Island

WASHINGTON

Columbia River

Missouri River

NORTH
DAKOTA

Long Beach
Peninsula

MONTANA

Missouri River

OREGON

Yellowstone River

South
Coast

IDAHO

SOUTH DAKOTA

Snake River

WYOMING

Sacramento River

Great
Salt Lake

NEBRASKA

Point
Reyes

NEVADA

Alcatraz
Island

UTAH

Colorado River

COLORADO

KANSAS

Monterey
to Big Sur

Arkansas

CALIFORNIA

Santa
Barbara

OKLAHOMA

Colorado River

Santa
Catalina
Island

ARIZONA

NEW MEXICO

Rio Grande

TEXAS

0   100   200   300 miles

ALASKA

Rio Grande

Kodiak
Island

0   200   400 miles

Padre
Island

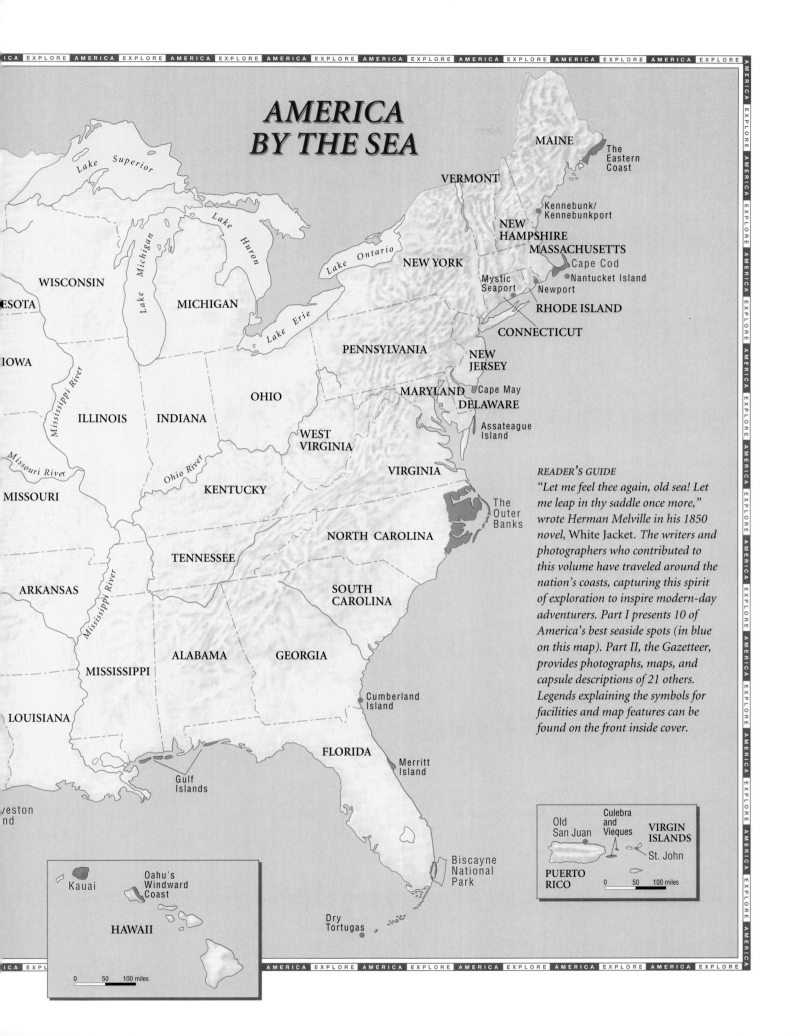

AMERICA BY THE SEA

MAINE

The Eastern Coast

VERMONT

Kennebunk/ Kennebunkport

NEW HAMPSHIRE

MASSACHUSETTS

Lake Superior

Lake Michigan

Lake Huron

Lake Ontario

NEW YORK

Cape Cod

Nantucket Island

WISCONSIN

Mystic Seaport

Newport

MICHIGAN

RHODE ISLAND

ESOTA

Lake Erie

CONNECTICUT

IOWA

PENNSYLVANIA

NEW JERSEY

Mississippi River

OHIO

MARYLAND

Cape May

DELAWARE

ILLINOIS

INDIANA

WEST VIRGINIA

Assateague Island

Missouri River

VIRGINIA

Ohio River

KENTUCKY

READER'S GUIDE

"Let me feel thee again, old sea! Let me leap in thy saddle once more," wrote Herman Melville in his 1850 novel, White Jacket. *The writers and photographers who contributed to this volume have traveled around the nation's coasts, capturing this spirit of exploration to inspire modern-day adventurers. Part I presents 10 of America's best seaside spots (in blue on this map). Part II, the Gazetteer, provides photographs, maps, and capsule descriptions of 21 others. Legends explaining the symbols for facilities and map features can be found on the front inside cover.*

MISSOURI

The Outer Banks

NORTH CAROLINA

ARKANSAS

Mississippi River

TENNESSEE

SOUTH CAROLINA

ALABAMA

GEORGIA

MISSISSIPPI

Cumberland Island

LOUISIANA

FLORIDA

Merritt Island

Gulf Islands

veston nd

Biscayne National Park

Kauai

Oahu's Windward Coast

Old San Juan

Culebra and Vieques

VIRGIN ISLANDS

St. John

PUERTO RICO

0   50   100 miles

HAWAII

Dry Tortugas

0   50   100 miles

CAPE COD

---

*Shaped by wind and sea, America's
most famous cape shelters a cache
of out-of-the-way treasures.*

Henry David Thoreau called Cape Cod "the
bare and bended arm of Massachusetts:
The shoulder is at Buzzard's Bay; the elbow, or
crazy bone, at Cape Mallebarre (the Old French
name for Cape Cod); the wrist at Truro; and the
sandy fist at Provincetown." An island since it
was severed from the mainland by the Cape Cod
Canal in 1916, Cape Cod juts more than 30 miles
into the Atlantic from the southeastern corner of
Massachusetts. The island's 300 miles of fine sand
beaches, backed in places by stretches of desert-
like dunes, ring a wooded interior sprinkled with
small lakes. The Cape's diverse towns include
Woods Hole, home to the world-famous oceanographic institute; aristocratic Chatham, with its
huge cedar-shingled "cottages" known as salt-
boxes; the historic summer hideaway of Wellfleet;
and colorful Provincetown, home of artists, poets,
and fishermen.

Cape Cod was formed from vast deposits of
sand and gravel left behind by retreating glaciers
during successive ice ages. In some places, glacial
debris buried huge chunks of ice, which eventually melted, causing the soil above to slump into

CEDAR SWAMP
The Atlantic White-Cedar Swamp, near Wellfleet, is home to a rare colony of this Southern coniferous tree. The species thrives in acid, peaty soils such as those of the Cape. Its dense stands form an impenetrable canopy that blocks light from reaching the forest floor.

INFORMATION FOR VISITORS

From Boston and northern New England, take Hwy. 3 to Sagamore Bridge; from Philadelphia, New York City, and Connecticut, take Hwys. 95, 195, and 495 to Hwy. 25, which leads to Bourne Bridge. Airports at Hyannis and Provincetown are both served by regularly scheduled flights. A round-trip passenger ferry runs daily between Boston and Provincetown in the summer. Ferries for Martha's Vineyard and Nantucket leave from Woods Hole (year-round) and Hyannis (summer only); a seasonal ferry operates between Martha's Vineyard and Nantucket. There are two visitor centers for Cape Cod National Seashore: the Salt Pond Visitor Center is located just north of Eastham on Hwy. 6; the Province Lands Visitor Center is located in Provincetown at the Cape's north end. In most areas, licenses are required for fishing and shellfishing.
For more information: Cape Cod Chamber of Commerce, Hyannis, MA 02061; 508-362-3225.

depressions known as kettle holes. Where the water table is near the surface, these concavities became the more than 365 kettle ponds that dot the Cape. Others were breached and drowned by the waters of the Atlantic, forming salty lagoons such as Salt Pond in Eastham.

For some 3,500 years, the peninsula has been inhabited by the Wampanoag Indians, a loose federation of tribes—including the Nauset, Pamet, Mashpee, and Mattakeese—that once fished the bountiful waters of Cape Cod Bay and grew maize and other crops. In 1627 Plymouth Pilgrims built Aptucxet, the first trading post in the New World at present-day Bourne and acted as middlemen between the Wampanoags and Dutch mariners in New Amsterdam. Starting in the 1630's settlers began to fell the forests, to farm, and to graze cattle and sheep. Cape Codders also turned their attention to the sea. Native oak and pine provided wood for schooners, barks, whalers, and packets. Fishing became a major means of livelihood for many towns and villages, with cod and mackerel among the most profitable catches. Although the harbors at Provincetown and Wellfleet were deep enough for whaling ships, it was the offshore island of Nantucket that would prosper most from the 19th-century whaling boom.

A SUMMER PLACE

In the last half of the 19th century, steamships and a railroad began to bring summer visitors from as far afield as Boston, Providence, and New York. At this time some 10,000 acres of the Cape were extensively

LOOK HOMEWARD, ANGEL
From rooftop balconies known as "widows' walks"—the example below being crowned by an angelic weather vane—Cape Cod wives awaited their husbands' return from the sea.

DUNE DEFENSE
Overleaf: Tenacious beach grasses clinging to a sand dune in Cape Cod National Seashore help to prevent erosion of the shoreline. Winds and waves are constantly reshaping the landscape of the Cape.

10

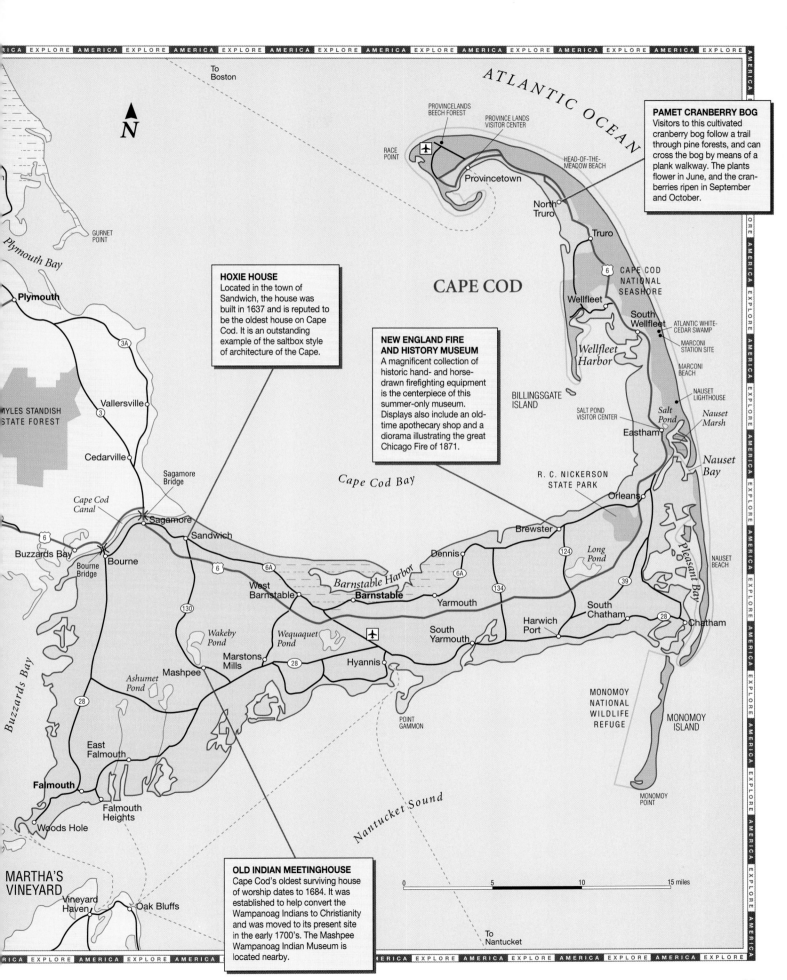

PAMET CRANBERRY BOG
Visitors to this cultivated cranberry bog follow a trail through pine forests, and can cross the bog by means of a plank walkway. The plants flower in June, and the cranberries ripen in September and October.

To Boston

N

PROVINCELANDS
BEECH FOREST

PROVINCE LANDS
VISITOR CENTER

RACE
POINT

Provincetown

HEAD-OF-THE-
MEADOW BEACH

North
Truro

Truro

6

CAPE COD
NATIONAL
SEASHORE

GURNET
POINT

Plymouth Bay

Plymouth

Wellfleet

South
Wellfleet

ATLANTIC WHITE-
CEDAR SWAMP

MARCONI
STATION SITE

MARCONI
BEACH

NAUSET
LIGHTHOUSE

HOXIE HOUSE
Located in the town of Sandwich, the house was built in 1637 and is reputed to be the oldest house on Cape Cod. It is an outstanding example of the saltbox style of architecture of the Cape.

CAPE COD

*Wellfleet
Harbor*

BILLINGSGATE
ISLAND

**NEW ENGLAND FIRE
AND HISTORY MUSEUM**
A magnificent collection of historic hand- and horse-drawn firefighting equipment is the centerpiece of this summer-only museum. Displays also include an old-time apothecary shop and a diorama illustrating the great Chicago Fire of 1871.

3A

SALT POND
VISITOR CENTER

*Salt
Pond*

*Nauset
Marsh*

Eastham

*Nauset
Bay*

MYLES STANDISH
STATE FOREST

Vallersville

3

Cedarville

*Cape Cod
Canal*

Sagamore
Bridge

Cape Cod Bay

R. C. NICKERSON
STATE PARK

Orleans

NAUSET
BEACH

Sagamore

Sandwich

Brewster

*Long
Pond*

124

*Pleasant
Bay*

Buzzards Bay

6

Bourne

Bourne
Bridge

6

6A

Dennis

6A

134

Barnstable Harbor

West
Barnstable

Barnstable

Yarmouth

South
Chatham

39

28

Chatham

130

Harwich
Port

*Wakeby
Pond*

*Wequaquet
Pond*

South
Yarmouth

Buzzards Bay

East
Falmouth

Marstons
Mills

28

Hyannis

*Ashumet
Pond*

Mashpee

28

Falmouth

MONOMOY
NATIONAL
WILDLIFE
REFUGE

MONOMOY
ISLAND

POINT
GAMMON

Falmouth
Heights

Woods Hole

MONOMOY
POINT

**MARTHA'S
VINEYARD**

Nantucket Sound

Vineyard
Haven

Oak Bluffs

OLD INDIAN MEETINGHOUSE
Cape Cod's oldest surviving house of worship dates to 1684. It was established to help convert the Wampanoag Indians to Christianity and was moved to its present site in the early 1700's. The Mashpee Wampanoag Indian Museum is located nearby.

To
Nantucket

0   5   10   15 miles

BEACH ROSE
Roses were originally planted on the Cape to help stabilize the sand dunes. Today wild roses, with their lavender-colored blossoms reaching two or three inches in diameter, thrive in many seashore areas.

CAPE ARCHITECTURE
The characteristic gray appearance of Cape Cod houses comes from the weathered cedar shingles used to sheathe the exterior.

planted with pitch pine and oak, successfully reversing two centuries of deforestation.

Today the now-leafy Cape is home to more than 190,000 year-round residents; in summer the population more than doubles. Two bridges over the Cape Cod Canal, at Bourne and Sagamore, provide access from the Massachusetts mainland to what is known as the Upper Cape. The Mid-Cape extends from Hyannis to Chatham, with the Lower Cape (or Outer Cape, according to some locals) jutting northward toward Provincetown.

The humpback Bourne Bridge deposits motorists from Massachusetts, Rhode Island, Connecticut, and New York on Highway 28, which goes down to the Cape's southern shore to link Falmouth, Woods Hole, and Hyannis—the latter two towns both ferry ports for Martha's Vineyard.

Although many visitors simply pass through Falmouth on their way to Martha's Vineyard, a detour to the Woods Hole Oceanographic Institute is well worth a side trip. In 1986 Woods Hole

scientists located the wreck of the ocean liner *Titanic* on the floor of the Atlantic Ocean off the coast of Newfoundland, and the institute presents fascinating exhibits on this discovery as well as the oceanographic research carried out here. Visitors can also tour the Marine Biological Laboratory, a unique facility housed in the 150-year-old Candle House, formerly used to store whale oil and make candles from spermaceti (a waxy substance derived principally from sperm whale oil).

Highlights of the Mid-Cape include Yarmouth, Dennis, Harwich Port—with its distinguished historic district—and lovely Chatham, fondly called the Cape's elbow. The town was settled in 1712 by William Nickerson. One of the most attractive towns on Cape Cod, Chatham is bordered by the Atlantic Ocean on the east side and by Nantucket Sound to the south. The town retains its strong links with the sea. Chatham Light, erected in 1877, stands on a bluff overlooking the ocean, and at Chatham Fish Pier, fishermen unload their boun-

ty of haddock, cod, flounder, lobster, and halibut caught in the offshore waters.

Other points of interest in Chatham include the Old Atwood House, built in 1752, and the historic Chatham Railroad Company Station, which offers displays of railroad memorabilia. The Old Grist Mill, built in 1797 to grind corn, offers public tours during July and August. And on Friday evenings in summer thousands of people picnic on the grassy hills surrounding the Chatham bandshell to listen to the town's brass ensemble. Amateur naturalists also flock here. From the town's harbor, excursion boats depart for Monomoy National Wildlife Refuge, just south of Chatham, where one of the greatest diversities of coastal birds in the eastern United States—some 285 species in all—gather on two uninhabited and windswept barrier islands. Migrating shorebirds, nesting waterfowl, and tern and gull colonies are to be found among the dunes, beaches, marshes, and scrub vegetation of this 2,700-acre refuge.

MOSSY BED
An exposed bed of peat moss, or sphagnum, is one of the unique natural features on Head-of-the-Meadow Beach, near Truro.

Sagamore Bridge connects Boston and northern New England with Highway 6, a limited-access four-lane highway that extends the 70-mile length of the peninsula. Running parallel to Highway 6 is pastoral Highway 6A, an old Indian trail known in colonial times as the King's Highway. This historic road is more scenic than Highway 6 and, on busy summer weekends, often less congested. It meanders along the shore of Cape Cod Bay, stitching together cranberry bogs, salt marshes, and white-steepled towns filled with antique shops and the characteristic Cape Cod houses—shingled, gray, and weatherbeaten—surrounded by picket fences.

HISTORIC TREASURES

The town of Sandwich is well worth a visit. This historic seaport was settled in the early 17th century, when it served as a trading post. Today its streets are lined with rows of modest clapboard houses and white Greek Revival mansions. The common, or village green, entices visitors to rest a while under the shady canopy of ancient trees before heading over to Dexter's Mill near Shawnee Pond. The gristmill operated from the 1650's until the late 19th century; today visitors can watch demonstrations of of old milling techniques. The Sandwich Glass Company thrived during the 19th century, producing glass in subtle shades of amber and gold and boosting the local economy. The Sandwich Glass Museum displays some of these man-made treasures, which are cherished by glass collectors for their lacy engraved designs.

PORCH PATRONS
The front porch of the Brewster Store—a former church that is one of the Cape's oldest general stores—is an ideal setting for conversation and rumination.

Along Gully Lane, just east of Sandwich, stands the Old Briar Patch, made famous by author Thornton W. Burgess as the home of Peter Rabbit. Born in Sandwich in 1874, the young Burgess was fond of exploring the pasture and woodland now protected in this conservation area. A self-guiding trail wanders through the dense thickets of bull briar that give the property its name. This woody vine provides a safe habitat for eastern cottontails (kin of Peter Rabbit), red foxes (Reddy Fox), and the other delightful small mammals that populate Burgess's books. A museum, housed in a 1756 home that once belonged to Burgess's aunt, Arabella Eldred Burgess, exhibits an extensive collection of Burgess's original manuscripts, as well as original illustrations for the books, which were done by Harrison Cady. The museum offers children's story hours during the summer.

The Cape Cod Museum of Natural History in Brewster provides a fascinating introduction to Cape Cod. The museum's 80-acre grounds include three nature trails that allow visitors to explore the Cape's different natural environments—salt marsh,

principal means of traveling to and from the Cape was by rail until a steamer service began operating between Provincetown and Boston.

THE LOWER CAPE

Beyond Orleans, Highway 6 continues north into the Lower Cape, a region dominated by the 27,000-acre Cape Cod National Seashore. The preserve's natural environments include bay and ocean beaches, salt and freshwater marshes, scrubby heathlands, and forests of oak, pitch pine, and red cedar. Six oceanfront beaches are protected within this region. The Salt Pond Visitor Center in Eastham is an ideal place to get acquainted with the seashore's natural and

FISHING FLEET
Provincetown's protected harbor, below, has sheltered fishing boats since colonial times. The town's fishermen still harvest the fishing grounds of Georges Bank.

cattail marsh, and beach. Brewster on Cape Cod Bay also has a large number of handsome sea captains' houses decorating its streets. The graves of mariners crowd the cemetery next to the First Parish Church, built in 1834 and known as the Captains' Church. This white clapboard church contains many pews that are still marked with the names of Brewster's famous sea captains.

Eight kettle ponds dot R. C. Nickerson State Park, located a few miles southeast of Orleans. Often called the jewel of the Massachusetts park system, this 2,700-acre reserve was once the estate of railroad baron Roland C. Nickerson and his wife, Addie, who donated the tract to the state in 1934. The following year the Civilian Conservation Corps planted 88,000 white pine, red pine, eastern hemlock, and spruce trees, which are now a paradise for thrushes, wrens, warblers, and other woodland birds. Open from April to November, the park offers picnicking, swimming, hiking, canoeing, sailing, fishing, and biking on an eight-mile stretch of the paved Cape Cod Rail Trail. The trail follows a section of the old railroad bed; until the 1920's the

TAIL OF A WHALE
With a wave of its tail, a diving humpback whale vanishes into the depths of the waters around Cape Cod. Now protected from hunting, whales were once the mainstay of Cape Cod's economy.

human history. From the visitor center, the mile-long Nauset Marsh Trail loops around Salt Pond then skirts past Nauset Marsh, where thousands of birds gather in summer.

The waves of Nauset Beach, the national seashore's southernmost sandspit, attract body and board surfers. Along the beach, boulders long ago cast aside by retreating glaciers are prime feeding areas (and consequently prime viewing areas) for common eiders and other wintering sea ducks.

The town of Wellfleet preserves the aura of 19th-century New England. In this tidy seaside village, churches send white spires above a leafy canopy, and quiet streets are lined with simple white clapboard cottages and black-shuttered Victorian sea captains' houses. The First Congregational Church steeple strikes "ship's time" with bells on the half hour, reminding visitors that this whaling port has long trusted in the sea. Wellfleet Harbor has been famous for its oysters since the 1600's.

On the Cape's Atlantic shore, an observation platform at the Marconi Station Site in Cape Cod National Seashore offers panoramic views of the peninsula, the Atlantic, and Cape Cod Bay. A stroll east from the platform leads to a 70-foot-high sea cliff, which overlooks Marconi Beach. Erosion has caused the cliff to retreat a considerable distance west since the turn of the century. The tower site from which Guglielmo Marconi sent the first transatlantic radio message on January 18, 1903, is now more than 200 feet out to sea.

ROOFTOP CATCH
A whimsical roof adornment proclaims the popularity of one of Cape Cod's most sought-after exports—the lobster.

North of Wellfleet, the Cape begins to hook westward. On the Atlantic side of Highway 6 in North Truro, the short Pilgrim Spring Trail leads to a freshwater spring reputedly used by the Pilgrims after they landed here in November 1620.

AT LAND'S END — Clasped in the clenched fist of Thoreau's "bare and bended arm," Provincetown is a cosmopolitan resort at the very tip of the Cape, a colorful enclave where smugglers congregated in the late 17th century, where 19th-century Portuguese whalers jumped ship, and where early 20th-century writers, poets, and artists found refuge. Eugene O'Neill, Tennessee Williams, Sinclair Lewis, and John Dos Passos all began their careers here. Charles W. Hawthorne led groups of

MIGHTY MONUMENT

*At the tip of the Cape, the granite
Pilgrim Monument—the nation's
tallest all-granite structure—towers
over the rooftops of Provincetown.*

SEASHORE SCALLOP

*Scallops form just a part of the
Cape's plethora of seafood. Offshore
shellfish beds and fishing grounds
also yield oysters, quahogs, mussels,
razor clams, and blue crabs.*

artists to paint the landscape around the town.
Hawthorne founded the Cape Cod School of Art in
Provincetown in 1899, which soon attracted
Edward Hopper and other painters.

The first unconventional types to pass this way
were the Pilgrims in 1620. The Pilgrim Monument,
a 257-foot granite tower, was erected in 1907 to
commemorate anchorage of the *Mayflower* in
Provincetown Harbor. The Provincetown Museum
at the base of the monument displays artifacts from
the pirate ship *Whydah*, skippered by the infamous
Samuel "Black Sam" Bellamy. On April 26, 1717,
the vessel sank in a wild storm off Wellfleet, where
it remains to this day.

Prosperous 19th-century homes survive along
Commercial Street. In the genteel East End, floral
and sculpture gardens and art galleries flank the
thoroughfares. MacMillan Pier is the headquarters
of the town's fishing industry; fishing and whale-
watching excursions leave from here.

Provincetown's picturesque streets and lanes present a startling contrast to the town's immediate
surroundings—desolate moors and windswept
sand dunes. These often forlorn expanses are now
preserved within the Province Lands section of the
national seashore. An observation deck at the
Province Lands Visitor Center near Race Point
provides spectacular views of the broad sweeping
ocean beaches in what is probably Cape Cod's most
dramatic landscape. Wind and the still-rising sea
continue to shape the region, eroding, transport-
ing, and depositing the Cape's glacial legacy. Here,
where the Pilgrims once trod, Cape Cod finally
gives way to the pounding Atlantic waves.

NEARBY SITES & ATTRACTIONS

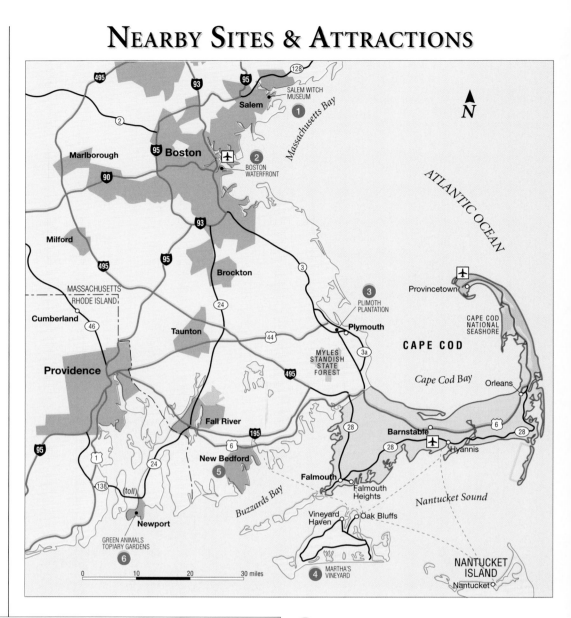

Just outside the modern town of Plymouth, Massachusetts, Plimoth Plantation faithfully re-creates the settlement established by the Pilgrims in 1620.

1 SALEM WITCH MUSEUM

Housed in an imposing former Unitarian church, the Salem Witch Museum brings to life the infamous Salem Witch Trials of 1692. When several young girls suffered fits and convulsions, accusations of witchcraft were leveled against a number of local townspeople. By means of life-size figures, stage sets, narration, and dramatic lighting, the museum's sound-and-light show re-creates the court proceedings that led to the execution of 20 Salem men and women as witches. The museum is open daily with presentations every half hour. Located on Washington Sq. in Salem.

2 BOSTON WATERFRONT

A blend of the old and the new makes Boston's Waterfront one of the city's liveliest areas. At the Boston Tea Party Ship and Museum, visitors can board a replica sailing vessel where costumed guides reenact the 1773 rebellion against excessive British taxation. The New England Aquarium on

Central Wharf houses hundreds of species of sea animals and an endearing colony of penguins. The aquarium boasts one of the largest seawater fish tanks in the world (180,000 gallons) in which sharks, salmon, and sea turtles can be viewed at close range. On Museum Wharf, the Computer Museum houses the world's largest two-story computer, where visitors can climb aboard a giant keyboard and run a software simulation on a 108-square-foot monitor. A virtual-reality exhibit lets participants "pilot" a flight simulator and race a sports car. At the nearby Boston Children's Museum, staff lead children on discovery activities that include a giant puzzle maze, treasure hunts, mask-making workshops, and games from other cultures. Located in downtown Boston.

3 PLIMOTH PLANTATION

This living museum of 17th-century Pilgrim life evokes the experience of the settlers who arrived on the *Mayflower* in 1620; a full-scale reproduction of the ship is docked in nearby Plymouth Harbor. Plymouth Rock is located in downtown Plymouth. Built on a hillside overlooking Cape Cod Bay and surrounded by a stockade, the plantation is a cluster of 15 simple wooden houses with thatched roofs. A fort, which also served as a meeting house, was built in 1622 to protect the settlement from attacks by local Indians. Costumed interpreters reenact daily activities such as musket drill, sheep shearing, baking in clay ovens, and salting fish. Many of the livestock kept at the site are the same breeds that the Pilgrims brought with them from England, including Iron Age pigs, and Devon cows. Plimoth Plantation is open daily from April through November. Located 2.5 miles south of Plymouth on Hwy. 3A.

4 MARTHA'S VINEYARD

Famous as a summer resort, Martha's Vineyard offers a mixture of rustic fishing villages, fertile farmland, and unspoiled natural areas. Roughly 20 miles long and 10 miles wide at its broadest point, the island's triangular shape is pierced by numerous inlets and bays, and dotted with saltwater ponds. The three main towns, Vineyard Haven, Edgartown, and Oak Bluffs, are served by ferries from the Cape. Edgartown was founded in 1642 and vied with Nantucket and New Bedford for control of the whaling trade. The town's Old Whaling Church is a reminder of its whaling days. Some of the extensive beaches on Martha's Vineyard are private, but Joseph Sylvia State Beach on Nantucket Sound and South Beach at Edgartown are open to the public. The highest point on the island is Little Peaked Hill, which rises 311 feet. Gay Head is home to one of only two Native American communities in Massachusetts. Nearby Cedar Tree Neck Wildlife Sanctuary is a haven for nature lovers, with 250 acres of woods, meadows, and beach. Located 7 miles off the southern tip of Cape Cod.

5 NEW BEDFORD

Renowned as the 19th-century whaling capital of the world, New Bedford is still a major deep-sea fishing port. At the height of the whaling boom of the 1840's and 1850's, New Bedford was among the wealthiest towns in the nation. Herman Melville immortalized New Bedford's hard-bitten mariners in *Moby Dick* and described vividly the houses of "perhaps the dearest place to live in all New England." Some of these historic houses, situated in the 14-block Waterfront District, have been restored and can be viewed on a walking tour of the area. The New Bedford Whaling Museum is a world-famous repository of whaling history, housing model sailing ships, harpoons, whaling tools, and scrimshaw—spermwhale teeth carved with intricate designs by sailors on long whaling voyages. The museum exhibits the whaling ship *Lagoda*, a fully rigged, half-scale replica that is the largest model ship in the world. Located east of Providence on Hwy. 195.

6 GREEN ANIMALS TOPIARY GARDENS

The art of topiary gardening—fashioning living plants such as boxwood, privet, and yew into the shapes of animals and geometric figures—is celebrated at this estate overlooking Narrangansett Bay in Portsmouth, Rhode Island. Green Animals was purchased by businessman Thomas E. Brayton in 1872. His love of horticulture led him to experiment with topiary gardening, assisted by his hardworking and imaginative gardener, Joseph Carreiro. Brayton's daughter, Alice—herself a horticulturist—named the garden Green Animals. Among the 80 pieces of topiary in the garden are more than 20 delightful animals—including a giraffe, camel, elephant, lion, ostrich, and peacocks—as well as many fine examples of geometric designs. The gardens are managed by the Preservation Society of Newport County. Located at 424 Bellevue Ave. in Newport.

The gracious summer homes of Martha's Vineyard, left, preserve the tranquil atmosphere that has made this island a favorite vacation hideaway for mainlanders.

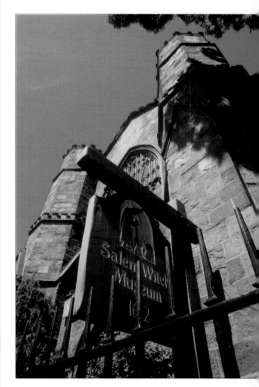

Salem's Witch Museum is a sobering reminder of the fear and suspicion that gripped the town during the infamous witch trials that took place here in 1692.

THE OUTER BANKS

These sandy sentinels shield North Carolina's historic coast from the onslaught of the Atlantic Ocean.

Few areas on earth have seen the fates mingle history, beauty, and recreation so cunningly as in the Outer Banks and their adjoining inland seas. Legendary capes add the luster of lonely lighthouses, epic shipwrecks, and booming sea battles. Mainland inlets hold quaint old seaport towns that once knew the power and might of royal governors and the swagger of rowdy pirates. Here the ocean wind sighed through the frail spindly confections of the Wright brothers, and the age of flight began.

From the Virginia border to Cape Fear, the long chain of windswept barrier islands of North Carolina is shaped like a great elbow that encloses the brackish waters of Albemarle Sound and Pamlico Sound. Together with the barrier islands, the deeply indented coastline of the sounds gives North Carolina the eighth-longest coastline in the nation.

These barrier islands were formed when nearshore currents washed eroded sediments along the state's gently sloping coast. In time these

OUTER BANKS OVERLOOK
Overleaf: At 200 feet high, spiral-painted Cape Hatteras Lighthouse is the tallest lighthouse in the U.S.

long sand banks were colonized by different species of plants whose seeds were washed up by the same currents that created the islands. The process continues, with currents constantly at work reshaping the shoreline.

Although barrier islands are a feature of much of the nation's southeastern coast, the Outer Banks are unique because they lie so far off the mainland. Experts speculate that the banks may be the remnants of an ancient shoreline that was breached when sea levels rose some 2,000 years ago. At that time the forested inland plains were flooded, forming the great inland seas of Albemarle and Pamlico.

THE FIRST COLONY

At the mouth of Albemarle Sound lies Roanoke Island. It was here that England managed to establish its first fragile foothold in the New World. Under the direction of Sir Walter Raleigh, two attempts were made to settle the northern tip of the island. Colonists were first sent out in 1585, but a settlement was not established until the summer of 1587. This second attempt to settle the island has lodged itself in American folklore as the Lost Colony.

After the colonists established themselves at Fort Raleigh, it was not until two years later that a ship

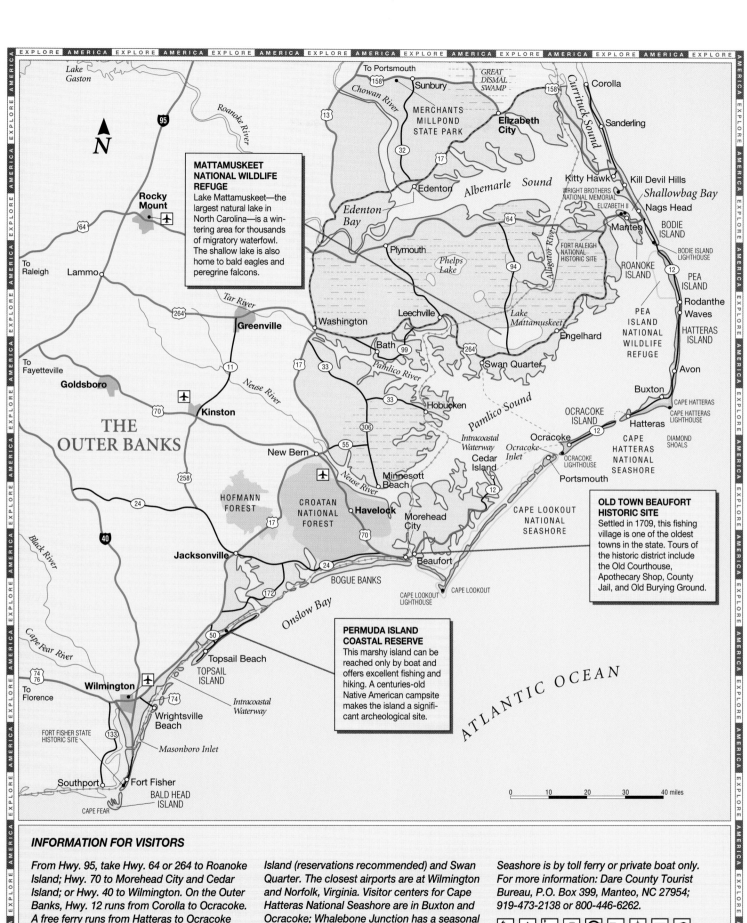

N

Lake Gaston

95

Roanoke River

Rocky Mount

64

To Raleigh

Lammo

264

Tar River

Greenville

11

To Fayetteville

Goldsboro

70

Kinston

THE OUTER BANKS

258

24

HOFMANN FOREST

40

CROATAN NATIONAL FOREST

Black River

Jacksonville

17

172

24

70

Neuse River

New Bern

55

306

33

Minnesott Beach

Havelock

Morehead City

BOGUE BANKS

Onslow Bay

50

Topsail Beach

TOPSAIL ISLAND

Intracoastal Waterway

Cape Fear River

74
76

To Florence

Wilmington

74

133

FORT FISHER STATE HISTORIC SITE

Wrightsville Beach

Masonboro Inlet

Southport

Fort Fisher

BALD HEAD ISLAND

CAPE FEAR

MATTAMUSKEET NATIONAL WILDLIFE REFUGE
Lake Mattamuskeet—the largest natural lake in North Carolina—is a wintering area for thousands of migratory waterfowl. The shallow lake is also home to bald eagles and peregrine falcons.

To Portsmouth

158

Sunbury

Chowan River

GREAT DISMAL SWAMP

MERCHANTS MILLPOND STATE PARK

13

32

17

Edenton

Edenton Bay

Plymouth

Washington

Bath

99

Pamlico River

33

Hobucken

Phelps Lake

94

Leechville

Lake Mattamuskeet

264

Swan Quarter

Engelhard

Pamlico Sound

Intracoastal Waterway

Cedar Island

Ocracoke Inlet

Minnesott Beach

Beaufort

CAPE LOOKOUT LIGHTHOUSE

CAPE LOOKOUT

CAPE LOOKOUT NATIONAL SEASHORE

158

Corolla

Currituck Sound

Sanderling

Elizabeth City

Albemarle Sound

Kitty Hawk

WRIGHT BROTHERS NATIONAL MEMORIAL

Kill Devil Hills

Shallowbag Bay

ELIZABETH II

Nags Head

Manteo

BODIE ISLAND

FORT RALEIGH NATIONAL HISTORIC SITE

ROANOKE ISLAND

BODIE ISLAND LIGHTHOUSE

12

PEA ISLAND

Rodanthe

Waves

HATTERAS ISLAND

Alligator River

Avon

Buxton

CAPE HATTERAS

CAPE HATTERAS LIGHTHOUSE

Hatteras

CAPE HATTERAS NATIONAL SEASHORE

DIAMOND SHOALS

OCRACOKE ISLAND

12

Ocracoke

OCRACOKE LIGHTHOUSE

Portsmouth

PEA ISLAND NATIONAL WILDLIFE REFUGE

OLD TOWN BEAUFORT HISTORIC SITE
Settled in 1709, this fishing village is one of the oldest towns in the state. Tours of the historic district include the Old Courthouse, Apothecary Shop, County Jail, and Old Burying Ground.

PERMUDA ISLAND COASTAL RESERVE
This marshy island can be reached only by boat and offers excellent fishing and hiking. A centuries-old Native American campsite makes the island a significant archeological site.

ATLANTIC OCEAN

0   10   20   30   40 miles

INFORMATION FOR VISITORS

From Hwy. 95, take Hwy. 64 or 264 to Roanoke Island; Hwy. 70 to Morehead City and Cedar Island; or Hwy. 40 to Wilmington. On the Outer Banks, Hwy. 12 runs from Corolla to Ocracoke. A free ferry runs from Hatteras to Ocracoke Island; from Ocracoke, ferries run to Cedar

Island (reservations recommended) and Swan Quarter. The closest airports are at Wilmington and Norfolk, Virginia. Visitor centers for Cape Hatteras National Seashore are in Buxton and Ocracoke; Whalebone Junction has a seasonal center. Access to Cape Lookout National

Seashore is by toll ferry or private boat only. For more information: Dare County Tourist Bureau, P.O. Box 399, Manteo, NC 27954; 919-473-2138 or 800-446-6262.

could sail from England with supplies. By the time the ship arrived, the fort was deserted. The only sign of the 112 colonists was the word, "CROATOAN"—the Powhatan name for Hatteras Island—carved into a post. The colony had agreed to join the Indians on Croatoan if they were forced to leave Roanoke. It is thought that calamity may have overtaken them quite suddenly, because the agreed sign of trouble—a Maltese cross—never was found.

The actual site of Fort Raleigh lies outside Manteo, Roanoke Island's 400-year-old harbor town. Here the National Park Service has reconstructed an approximation of the square fort of 1585. Each summer a long-running outdoor drama called *The Lost Colony* brings to life the story of the settlers' journey to the New World. Adjacent

CRAB CONVENTION
For crab lovers, the Outer Banks offers a veritable feast, above. Whether from a dock, a pier, or a beach, crabbing is a popular way to collect an inexpensive and tasty beach supper.

WORKING HARBOR
In Ocracoke harbor, right, neatly stacked crab pots hint at the occupation of many of the islanders. Fishing and crabbing provide two of the community's major sources of income. Ocracoke Lighthouse, in the background, is the oldest continually operating lighthouse in North Carolina.

to the fort and its outdoor amphitheater is the Elizabethan Gardens—a horticultural masterpiece—where beds of flowers lined with boxwood hedges are shaded by ancient live oaks, one of which may predate the Lost Colony itself. Moored in Manteo Harbor is *Elizabeth II*, a replica of an Elizabethan sailing ship. Aboard the ship, costumed crewmen reply to questions in rich Devonshire accents and remind visitors that the colonists' voyage from England took more than three months.

By a quirk of fate, the site picked by Wilbur and Orville Wright for their historic breakthrough was a mere 15 miles from the site of Raleigh's ill-starred colony. Because of the Outer Banks' steady winds, the Wrights chose what is now the town of Kill Devil Hills for their epochal experiments in powered flight. Thanks to the National Park Service,

the setting is one of the best interpreted of any of America's historic venues. It's inspiring to stroll along the path where the brothers launched glider warmups from a giant dune called Big Kill Devil Hill, and to encounter the four granite boulders that mark the termination of each of the successful takeoffs and landings made on December 17, 1903. The first flight covered only 120 feet and lasted a mere 12 seconds.

SOUTH TO HATTERAS	Today Kill Devil Hills is alive with development, as are its neighbors, Kitty Hawk and Nags Head. Not far away, there

is another Outer Banks. Crossing the bridge from Manteo, visitors can glimpse stunted shrubbery and dark green clumps of pine trees, vast flat expanses of tan sea marsh, and dignified formations of pelicans. The natural heart of the Banks asserts itself still more strongly to the south in the chain of islands that comprises the 30,310-acre Cape Hatteras National Seashore.

For 80 miles along the coast, the barrier chain is preserved in its pristine state. There is a scattering

SMOOTH AS A MILL POND
A world away from the sandy Outer Banks, bald cypress trees rise from the tannin-stained waters of Merchants Millpond State Park, above, located near Sunbury, north of Albemarle Sound.

of commercial developments around old towns such as Rodanthe, Waves, Avon, and Buxton. Modern marinas are geared to ocean sportfishing; hang gliders and kite flyers share the sky. Roadside pullouts, bird-watching platforms, and wildlife trails beckon the visitor to savor the freshness of the coast. The Pea Island National Wildlife Refuge is a good place to pull off the road, head for the beachfront, and swim in an ocean that is much the same as it was when the Elizabethans anchored here. Starting perhaps 400 yards out, the combers roll in with long booms of lazy power, twirling clouds of sand inside them as they curl, churning a taupe-hued lather that hisses dying onto the beach. Just a small demonstration of the ocean's power suggests a larger potential for danger. Cape Hatteras is known with good reason as the Graveyard of the Atlantic: this stretch of coast has swallowed up an estimated 600 ships since records have been kept.

Looking out to sea on a bright summer day, it is difficult to conjure up the grim history of these sparkling waters. Yet a close look to the southeast toward Diamond Shoals reveals the tumultuous flashes of whitecaps—very different from the calm ultramarine blue of the deeper ocean to the north. In the ocean off Hatteras lie shipwrecks of every era. Here U.S. destroyers battled German submarines in "Torpedo Junction" during World War II. In 1862 the legendary Union ironclad *Monitor* went down following its battle with the Confederate ironclad *Merrimac* at Hampton Roads.

The graveyard's most famous monument—Cape Hatteras Lighthouse—rises just south of the town of Buxton. Dreamlike and immense against the clouds, the black-and-white-striped lighthouse stands 208 feet above the dunes. Climbing the 268 black-painted cast-iron steps to the top of Cape Hatteras Lighthouse is almost an obligatory ritual for any able-bodied person who has traveled this far. The view from the windswept observation platform is breathtaking, as the ocean thrashes up pools of frothing teal green near the base of the venerable tower. In 1871, when the light was first lit, 1,500 feet of sand lay between the lighthouse and the sea; one recent unofficial estimate put the water within 50 feet of the lighthouse today. The eroding shore may dictate that the giant structure be moved back to safer terrain.

Ocracoke Island is one part of the Outer Banks that motorists can reach only by ferry. Highway 12, which begins at Corolla near the Virginia border, continues along Ocracoke's 14-mile length. The village of Ocracoke has been home to seamen, fishermen, and pilots for centuries, and was a favorite haunt of the infamous pirate Edward Teach, better known as Blackbeard. In 1718 Ocracoke Inlet was the site of the bloody engagement during which Lt. Robert Maynard of the Royal Navy—under orders from Virginia's royal governor, Alexander Spotswood—killed Blackbeard in hand-to-hand combat. Maynard mounted the pirate's severed head on the bowsprit of his ship, *Ranger*, and sailed back to Virginia.

Beyond Ocracoke lies Cape Lookout National Seashore, a wild and roadless string of islands. Cape Lookout's only settlement—Portsmouth Village, just across Ocracoke Inlet—was an important port during the 1700's but is now deserted. From Portsmouth to Beaufort Inlet runs a landscape of grassy sand dunes, with the lighthouse at Cape Lookout warning mariners away from another of the Outer Banks' shipping graveyards.

TREASURES OF THE SOUNDS

Perhaps Blackbeard should have stayed at his other favorite residence, the mainland port town of Bath, located to the west across Pamlico Sound. According to local legend, Blackbeard enjoyed the protection of yet another Bath resident, Gov. Charles Eden, who allegedly took a share of the pirate's booty. Today the entire village of Bath is on the National Register of Historic Places. A walking tour from the Historic Bath Visitor Center winds through streets draped with pecan and myrtle trees, taking in such landmarks as St. Thomas Church of 1734—the oldest standing church in the state—and the 1751 Palmer-Marsh House, whose unusual double chimney covers almost one whole end of the house.

Bath is just one of a number of charming port towns on the mainland coast, an area that differs in virtually every way from the Outer Banks. This is a region of dark forests, deeply indented by freshwater bays, inlets, and swamps. West of the sounds, the wilderness gradually gives way to broad fields of corn and peanuts.

The combination of farming and seaborne trade brought prosperity to Bath and its northern neighbor, Edenton, which captures the past centuries in its historic buildings. From the Cupola House of 1758 to the tiny 1890's business district, Edenton is a textbook of American architecture. In front of one ancient house, a bronze teapot mounted on a vertical cannon barrel presents an incongruous sight. The monument honors local women who in 1774 vowed to drink no more English tea, a historic boycott known as the Edenton Tea Party.

Edenton never grew much beyond its original 18th-century form. Not so its rival to the south, New Bern, founded in 1710 by Swiss and German colonists on an arm of Pamlico Sound. The town's central location made it an obvious place for pre-Revolutionary North Carolina's first permanent capital. New Bern's combined capitol and gover-

nor's residence, Tryon Palace, was completed in 1770. After the Revolution it served as the first North Carolina state capitol, until the seat of government was moved to Raleigh. Destroyed by fire in 1798, Tryon Palace was fully restored in the 1950's according to the original architect's plans. A building that bespeaks the peak years of Georgian grace and elegance, it holds one of the country's great collections of decorative arts.

STILT-LEGGED COTTAGES
Beach homes near Nags Head, below, attest to the popularity of the Outer Banks as a vacation destination. Wind-whipped stands of sea oats and other grasses help bind the shifting sands beneath the post-propped houses along the shore.

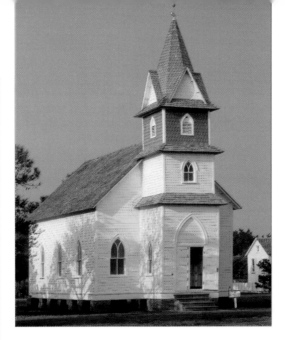

VILLAGE MEMORIES
The immaculately maintained Methodist church at Portsmouth Village, right, on Ocracoke Inlet in Cape Lookout National Seashore, is a poignant reminder of former times in this deserted hamlet. Founded in 1753, Portsmouth was once an important port, where oceangoing vessels would unload their cargo onto smaller craft for shipment to mainland ports. When shoals made the inlet impassable during the late 1800's, Portsmouth fell into decline.

CITY STORIES

Guided tours cover New Bern's architectural and historic treasures. In one yard a soaring cypress tree is said to have shaded patriots' meetings before the Revolution. In a brick mansion nearby, Union general Ambrose Burnside made his headquarters during the Union army's occupation. On one street a local pharmacist invented Pepsi-Cola; on another stands a palatial Depression-era post office built by the Works Progress Administration (WPA).

New Bern is approximately halfway down the North Carolina coast. The remaining half is the land of Cape Fear and the history-drenched city of Wilmington. The region is outlined by a chain of barrier islands set close to the mainland.

Knowledgeable locals say the star of the south is Wrightsville Beach, an island just minutes from Wilmington. Its oceanfront is blessed with a gentle surf; the offshore currents often touch its famously clear water with shades of Caribbean blue. Somehow Wrightsville Beach has resisted many of the temptations of beach commercialization, and remains an area of family cottages. Loggerhead sea turtles come ashore to nest in the sands of the leading beachfront hotel. From a picturesque harbor on the sheltered side, Masonboro Inlet gives fishermen fast access to the Atlantic.

From its incorporation in 1739, Wilmington was a key port, but during the Civil War it became the Confederacy's main haven for blockade runners—fast steamers that slipped out under the very noses of blockading Union ships to trade cotton and tobacco to the British for arms and supplies. For most of the war the port was kept open by the guns of Fort Fisher, a massive earthwork fort built in 1861. The fort's remains are open to the public, and a small museum at the site displays items recovered from sunken blockade runners. When Wilmington fell, the South's hopes ended.

South of Wilmington, Cape Fear marks the end of the journey. Taking its name from the trepidation it inspired among 16th-century mariners, Cape Fear lies on Bald Head Island—accessible by ferry from mainland Southport. Private ownership has preserved the island's natural charms. Careful local stewardship ensures that this corner of the Outer Banks will continue to safeguard its treasures.

FISHERMAN'S WHARF
One of three fishing piers within the Cape Hatteras National Seashore, Hatteras Island pier, below, is favored by anglers and visitors alike. The Outer Banks' 100 miles of unspoiled oceanfront offer unlimited opportunities for surf fishing.

NEARBY SITES & ATTRACTIONS

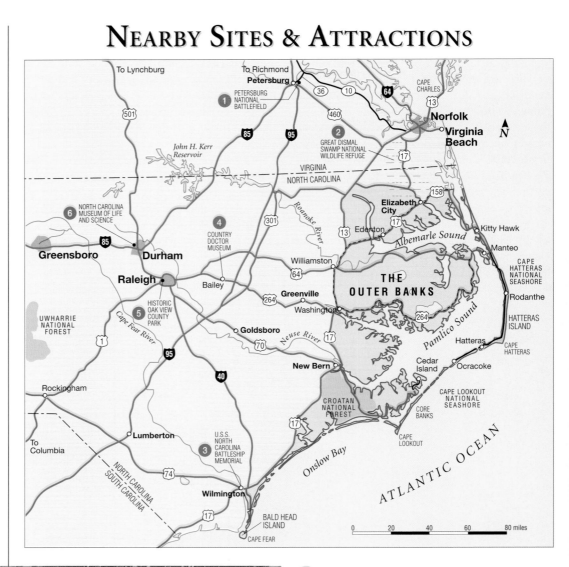

This gracious Greek Revival farmhouse at Historic Oak View County Park provides a glimpse into the leisured lifestyle of a wealthy North Carolina cotton planter.

1 PETERSBURG NATIONAL BATTLEFIELD

In the summer of 1864, the Confederate army was pinned down at Petersburg, enduring a siege that lasted from June 1864 to April 1865. Petersburg National Battlefield preserves the site of those bloody battles. The battlefield includes miles of siege lines, several cannon-lined forts, and the huge crater left behind when Union forces set off a gigantic mine under the Confederate defenses on July 30, 1864. At the visitor center, a three-dimensional map of the 2,700-acre site explains the different phases of the long onslaught. During the summer months, costumed interpreters carry out artillery demonstrations. There is also a reconstructed Union siege encampment and field hospital; the latter includes a surgeon's tent, complete with instruments. Earthworks and a winter quarters have also been reconstructed. Located 2½ miles east of Petersburg on Hwy. 36.

2 GREAT DISMAL SWAMP NATIONAL WILDLIFE REFUGE

Dense stands of black gum, cypress, pine, and juniper trees grow on islands amid the intricate maze of creeks and bogs that make up Great Dismal Swamp. Dominated by Lake Drummond, this

107,000-acre wetland is fed by numerous intermittent streams. Tannic acid, released from the peat of trees, turns the water a reflective brown while also purifying it. White-tailed deer, gray and red foxes, and otters are commonly sighted in the refuge, and the rich foliage is home to hundreds of bird species. The swamp's wild residents are most easily spotted from the boat and canoe routes that lead to Lake Drummond, as well as from a boardwalk that winds through the forest. Fishing is permitted only in Lake Drummond, where catfish, speckle, and bluegill are abundant. Located south of Norfolk off Hwy. 17.

③ U.S.S. *NORTH CAROLINA* BATTLESHIP MEMORIAL

Now a memorial for all North Carolina veterans of World War II, the U.S.S. *North Carolina* served in every major phase of the war in the Pacific, including the battles of Guadalcanal and Iwo Jima, earning 15 battle stars by war's end. Nine decks are open to visitors; a self-guided tour includes the galley, sick bay, engine room, pilot house, crew's quarters, mess hall, machine shop, and officers' staterooms, as well as the massive gun turrets. On the main deck is a restored Kingfisher floatplane. The ship's museum shows a short film on the history of the ship, and displays photographs and artifacts from its career in World War II. Located off Hwy. 17.

④ COUNTRY DOCTOR MUSEUM

The offices of two 19th-century country doctors were joined to create this unique museum. Displays include a replica of an 1850's apothecary, which contains a drug counter with medicines stored on cherrywood shelves. The doctor's office displays many items used by country doctors over the years, including a jar of preserved leeches and instruments used in dental operations and childbirth. Highlighting the collection are the instruments used to amputate the arm of Civil War hero Stonewall Jackson. Behind the museum is an herb garden that grows 20 different medicinal herbs used by doctors at the turn of the century. A 1912 Ford automobile on display reminds visitors that country doctors often needed to travel long distances to care for their patients. Located in Bailey on Hwy. 264.

⑤ HISTORIC OAK VIEW COUNTY PARK

The history of cotton is showcased at Historic Oak View County Park, which interprets the agricultural heritage of Wake County from its antebellum days to the 1940's. The site includes a Greek Revival–style farmhouse, detached kitchen, barn, gazebo, herb garden, and a 1900 cotton gin barn that houses a museum. Artifacts and photographs tell the story of what for many decades was North Carolina's most important crop. Visitors can gin cotton and see the cotton plants growing in a field outside the museum. A grove of pecan trees planted in the early 1900's surrounds the farmstead, which is listed on the National Register of Historic Places. There are annual displays of agricultural tools, and workshops are offered in historic crafts. Located 3 miles east of Raleigh off Hwy. 440.

⑥ NORTH CAROLINA MUSEUM OF LIFE AND SCIENCE

Scientific discovery and the natural history of North Carolina are the focus of this eclectic museum, which features both indoor and outdoor displays. Visitors board a train for a 1-mile ride through outdoor attractions that include the farmyard exhibit, comprised of five farm buildings and a petting area—with goats, sheep, pigs, rabbits, and a donkey—and the nature park, featuring a close look at animals native to North Carolina, such as a cougar, bobcat, bison, black bears, and red wolves. The museum's indoor exhibits include a full-scale re-creation of a lunar landing site, as well as a moon rock, rocket engines, and actual flight suits. At the geology exhibit, an interactive videodisk puts visitors inside a volcano or on earth during prehistoric times. A weather exhibit includes radar and live weather satellite data, as well as a 13-foot-high tornado in a controlled environment. Located at 433 Murray Ave. in Durham.

Rows of jars in the apothecary area of the Country Doctor Museum contain medicines used by country doctors. This replica of a 19th-century pharmacy also displays a unique collection of medical books and doctors' diaries.

Silenced by time, a weathered bronze cannon stands in Petersburg National Battlefield. During the long siege of Petersburg, more than 70,000 Union and Confederate soldiers were killed, wounded, or died of disease.

BISCAYNE NATIONAL PARK

*North America's only living coral
reef is the vibrant centerpiece
of this undersea preserve.*

On the southeastern edge of the North American continent, an underwater wonderland unfolds in the clear waters of Biscayne Bay, located just 30 miles south of Miami. Here iridescent tropical fish dart among forests of brightly colored coral, gentle manatees swim slowly among the turtle grass beds near shore, and great blue herons pose motionless in the shallows adjacent to the coastal mangrove forests. In this picture-perfect marine world, all signs of civilization seem a world away.

An oceanfront park 17 miles long without any beaches, Biscayne National Park is a pristine paradise for marine life and birds, as well as snorkelers, divers, and fishermen. The park's total of 181,000 acres extends from the rim of the mainland to approximately seven miles into the Atlantic off Elliott Key, Sands Key, and Ragged Keys. To anyone with a boat, it's open and accessible, with only a handful of restricted areas. From the vantage point of a glass-bottom boat, visitors can get an eyeful of Biscayne's

COLORFUL CRUSTACEAN
The park's underwater landscape is home to a multitude of intriguing marine life, including this banded coral shrimp, seen here crawling across a vibrant purple sponge.

main attraction—the northernmost section of North America's only living coral reef.

Among the 48 national parks administered by the National Park Service, Biscayne National Park is the only one that is 95 percent water. Biscayne preserves a unique subtropical coastal habitat for the animals and plants that thrive both under and above the water. The park consists of four distinct but interconnected ecosystems: the mangrove coastline, the bay itself, a string of offshore barrier islands, and the open ocean reefs.

Established first as a national monument in 1968 and upgraded to national park status in 1980, Biscayne is a strategically placed natural buffer that protects an environmentally sensitive area of crowded South Florida. The city of Miami lies on its northern boundary; the Florida Keys marine sanctuary abuts its southern border; and Everglades National Park is just 21 miles to the west. The park contains the best elements of both the Keys and the Everglades and has suffered few blemishes from any human development.

Biscayne's 26 miles of mangroves are the longest stretch of unbroken mangrove coastline remaining on Florida's east coast. These salt-tolerant trees, with their characteristic branching prop roots, grow in shallow waters along the seashore. Much of South Florida was lined with mangroves just a century ago, but the trees were eventually removed in many places to make the waterfront more appealing for development.

Yet mangroves play a critical role in the vitality of Biscayne Bay. The dominant species is the red mangrove, which juts out from shore to grow right in the bay. The mazelike red roots of these trees emerge above the water by as much as three or four feet from their slender trunks. The underwater root tangle provides hiding places and a secure nursery for shrimp, crabs, lobsters, and small gamefish. Raccoons also frequent mangroves in search of oysters (known as "coon oysters") that grow in clusters on the roots.

SHALLOW WATERS

Biscayne's mangroves sit at the edge of one of the park's most important but least understood biological zones—the hardbottom. This is the heart and soul of shallow Biscayne Bay, which averages only eight feet deep. The hardbottom is classified as an area with less than an inch of sediment atop the underlying limestone rock. In Biscayne Bay, mats of green turtle grass take root where sediment has built up in depressions in the hardbottom, making the crystal-clear water appear at first glance to be dull and flat.

Scrape away some of the sediment, however, and what is revealed is a limestone base that resembles

REEF ROVERS
Overleaf: Redband parrotfish patrolling the coral reefs use their powerful jaws and razor-sharp teeth to chew up hardened coral and extract the edible algae from it.

INFORMATION FOR VISITORS

The main entrance to Biscayne National Park is Convoy Point Information Station, site of the park headquarters and main visitor center, located east of Homestead on North Canal Dr. (SW 328 St.). To get to Convoy Point from Miami, take the Florida Tpk. (Homestead Ext.) and then Tallahassee Rd. (SW 137 Ave.) to North Canal Dr.; from the Florida Keys, take Hwy. 1 to Homestead and then North Canal Dr. The nearest major airport is in Miami. Within the park, visitor centers on Adams Key, Elliott Key, and Boca Chita Key may be reached only by boat; all offer free boat docking facilities. Glass-bottom boat tours of Biscayne Bay, the islands, and the offshore reefs—run by a park concessioner—leave from Convoy Point.
For more information: Biscayne National Park, P.O. Box 1369, Homestead, FL 33090-1369; 305-247-PARK.

MILD-MANNERED MAMMAL
With its walruslike head, barrel-shaped torso, and broad, flat tail, the gentle manatee presents a startling sight. The air-breathing mammal has no back legs; its front legs have evolved into flippers for swimming.

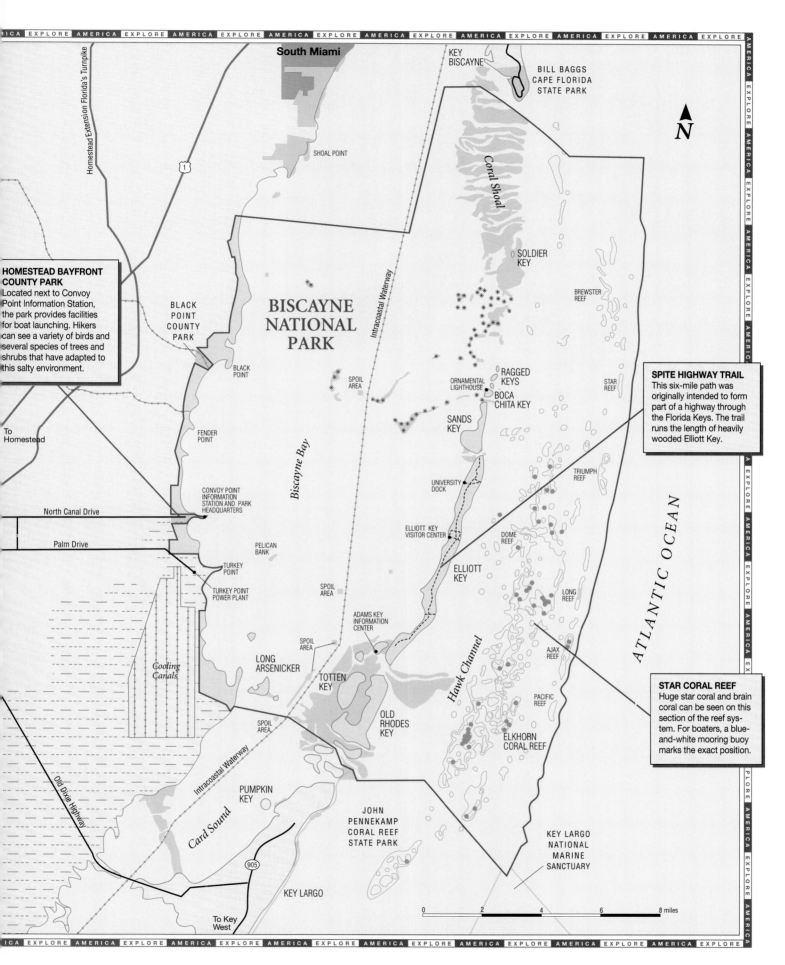

South Miami

KEY BISCAYNE

BILL BAGGS CAPE FLORIDA STATE PARK

Homestead Extension Florida's Turnpike

Coral Shoal

SHOAL POINT

N

U.S. 1

BISCAYNE NATIONAL PARK

Intracoastal Waterway

SOLDIER KEY

BREWSTER REEF

HOMESTEAD BAYFRONT COUNTY PARK

Located next to Convoy Point Information Station, the park provides facilities for boat launching. Hikers can see a variety of birds and several species of trees and shrubs that have adapted to this salty environment.

BLACK POINT COUNTY PARK

BLACK POINT

SPOIL AREA

ORNAMENTAL LIGHTHOUSE

RAGGED KEYS

BOCA CHITA KEY

STAR REEF

SPITE HIGHWAY TRAIL

This six-mile path was originally intended to form part of a highway through the Florida Keys. The trail runs the length of heavily wooded Elliott Key.

To Homestead

FENDER POINT

Biscayne Bay

SANDS KEY

CONVOY POINT INFORMATION STATION AND PARK HEADQUARTERS

North Canal Drive

TRIUMPH REEF

UNIVERSITY DOCK

Palm Drive

PELICAN BANK

ELLIOTT KEY VISITOR CENTER

DOME REEF

ATLANTIC OCEAN

TURKEY POINT

TURKEY POINT POWER PLANT

SPOIL AREA

ELLIOTT KEY

LONG REEF

ADAMS KEY INFORMATION CENTER

SPOIL AREA

Cooling Canals

LONG ARSENICKER

SPOIL AREA

AJAX REEF

STAR CORAL REEF

Huge star coral and brain coral can be seen on this section of the reef system. For boaters, a blue-and-white mooring buoy marks the exact position.

TOTTEN KEY

OLD RHODES KEY

Hawk Channel

PACIFIC REEF

Old Dixie Highway

Intracoastal Waterway

PUMPKIN KEY

Card Sound

ELKHORN CORAL REEF

JOHN PENNEKAMP CORAL REEF STATE PARK

KEY LARGO NATIONAL MARINE SANCTUARY

905

KEY LARGO

0   2   4   6   8 miles

To Key West

EXPLORE AMERICA EXPLORE AMERICA EXPLORE AMERICA EXPLORE AMERICA EXPLORE AMERICA EXPLORE AMERICA EXPLORE AMERICA EXPLORE AMERICA EXPLORE AMERICA EXPLORE

BISCAYNE NATIONAL PARK 35

TROPICAL PLUMAGE
The mangroves and islands of Biscayne National Park are home to at least 179 species of birds, including this painted bunting that sports its blue, red, and green feathers.

a great cluster of fish eggs. Known as oolite, or egg stone, this granular rock was formed when South Florida sank into the sea and then re-emerged—a process that has occurred at least four times in recent geologic history. Each time that the land disappeared, millions of plants and animals perished, decomposed, and deposited calcium car-

bonate on the sea floor. The calcium carbonate hardened around grains of sand, creating oolite.

Solution holes, or pits, are common in this limestone rock. Fish and lobster use these minicraters as hiding places, as do brittle starfish and shrimp. Stone crabs and a surprising number of other species also live in the hardbottom zone.

The most sought-after hardbottom resident is the spiny lobster, easily distinguished from the cold-water variety of the Northeast by its absence of claws. For its first nine months of life, a spiny lobster remains in the larval stage as a transparent oval with legs. At nine months, when it reaches the size of a quarter, it settles into the hardbottom zone, where its real growth begins. If it's smart it will stay there, too, since lobstering is not permitted in Biscayne Bay—only on the outer reefs. The hardbottom also provides a safe nursery for young fish as they migrate offshore to the coral reefs. The region's carpet of turtle grass is a haven for some of Florida's most endangered animals, the largest and most famous of which is the manatee. Only 1,200 manatees are estimated to exist in the southeastern United States, living in Florida year-round.

The manatee's jowly face, adorned with spiky whiskers, somewhat resembles a walrus as does its girth. A fully grown manatee can be of awesome dimensions—well over 3,000 pounds and almost

13 feet in length. Although imposing in size, the manatee is shy and reclusive, and completely harmless to humans. It eats nothing but aquatic plants. Because these gentle creatures frequent coastal waters, many manatees unfortunately bear the scars of collisions with powerboats.

Sea turtles also visit Biscayne Bay to graze on the rich beds of turtle grass. Loggerhead, green, and hawksbill turtles are most frequently sighted in summer when these endangered creatures crawl onto Florida's beaches after dark to lay their eggs. Biscayne's mangrove-lined mainland is unsuitable for nesting, so the turtles use several sandy areas on the offshore islands.

Anglers, too, are drawn to the shallow bay in search of the nation's most prized gamefish—the bonefish. Although those of Biscayne Bay typically are not as numerous as those in the Keys, they have a reputation for being larger. As bottom feeders, bonefish are strong, fast swimmers that feast on crabs and clams.

THE BARRIER ISLANDS

Because so much of the park is water, the 42 barrier islands near Biscayne's eastern edge are easily overlooked. A complete world in themselves, the islands are the tips of ancient reefs, which emerged following the last ice age. Imprints of fossilized corals are present in the rocks on the islands, accessible only by boat.

As on the mainland, thick mangroves line much of the islands' shores. There are occasional sandy stretches but no true beaches. In the islands' interiors, however, grow tall hardwood forests that are more characteristic of the West Indies than of Florida. Jamaican dogwood, strangler fig, and a few stands of mahogany cover these junglelike islands, sprung from seeds carried here by the winds, on the waves, and in the digestive tracts of migrating birds.

One of the more easily recognized species is the gumbo limbo tree. Locals also jokingly refer to it as the "tourist tree," since at the end of a day in the Florida sun, the skin of careless visitors glows just as brightly as the tree's characteristic red bark.

Many of the trees on the islands—mahogany in particular—were cut down first by Indians, and then by Bahamians in search of timber to make boats. On Elliott Key, settlers cleared the forest to grow pineapples and limes. Ironically, the thick foliage of Elliott Key today is one of the last strongholds of the rare Schaus swallowtail and the zebra butterfly. Elliott Key and Boca Chita Key have the only camping facilities anywhere in the park, and there are also hiking trails through the forest. Campers and hikers typically visit only from

TENDER BLOSSOM
The flowering devil's-potato presents a delicate counterpoint to the tangle of the tropical forest.

BAYSIDE VIEW
A pleasure boat skims across the turquoise waters of Biscayne Bay, with the forested shoreline of Elliott Key visible on the horizon.

COASTAL GROVE

The intricate branching roots of mangrove trees shelter a great variety of marine creatures. Mangroves also prevent shoreline erosion and shield inland areas from the force of tropical storms.

December through April. Mosquitoes are so thick the rest of the year that the park's excursion boats avoid the islands entirely, and even recreational boaters tend not to tarry.

THE REEF WORLD

During the winter, several of Biscayne's islands—particularly Boca Chita Key, with its ornamental stone lighthouse—are popular destinations both for boaters and for those preparing to dive the most visually spectacular and most heavily inhabited part of Biscayne: the coral reefs. Authorities differ as to whether the reef system officially ends here or farther north off West Palm Beach. South of Biscayne, another section of the reef is preserved within John Pennekamp Coral Reef State Park.

Like the mangrove and hardbottom communities, the deepwater reefs are important gamefish nurseries as well as the chief residence of bottom dwellers such as snapper and grouper. But for sheer beauty, few can compare to the brightly colored tropical fish, especially the plate-sized, neon-glowing queen or French angelfish. Biscayne's coral reefs start in relatively shallow waters—only 15 feet to 20 feet deep. These reefs, seemingly as solid and unyielding as mountain granite, are among the world's most spectacular natural wonders. The massive stands of elkhorn and staghorn corals mimic the racks of game animals with uncanny precision. Other corals resemble trees and fans, so delicate in appearance that they seem far too fragile to exist, that the slightest wave action might rip them apart. The reason that coral colonies assume

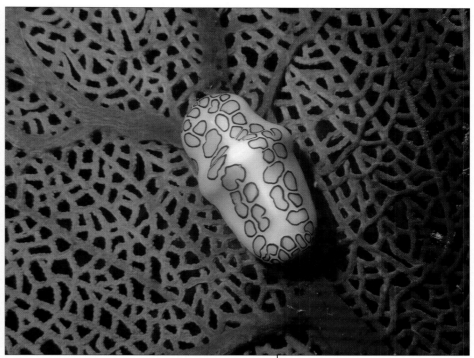

tiny creatures known as polyps. The growth rate is extremely slow because size increases only when one life cycle ends and a new one begins. Even then, growth is defined in terms of inches per decade.

Hard coral polyps attach themselves to the outer layer of coral formations, secreting calcium carbonate. These tiny polyps are usually hidden inside their skeletons during the day. They look much like squat sea anemones and, in fact, are closely related. The polyps usually appear only after dark, emerging to feed with their tentacles, which send out small stinging threads to paralyze and kill minute prey. These venomous threads are so small and weak that most people hardly ever notice them, with one important exception: fire coral, a species that richly deserves its name. This dark orange coral has stinging cells that produce a burning sensation when touched. When the coral polyps are feeding, the reef becomes a miniature forest of waving off-white, yellow, and bright orange filaments. In cracks and under crevices in the reef live crabs, shrimps, sponges, and a multitude of other animals that all depend on the coral polyps for their well-being.

Unlike hard coral, soft coral formations such as sea whips, sea feathers, sea plumes, and sea fans are plantlike in appearance. The polyps have eight tentacles and often feed during daytime hours. Their waving fronds provide shelter for many species of reef fish, including blue-striped grunts.

It could easily be argued that the coral reef is Florida's greatest natural asset. Visitors continue to flock to Biscayne National Park to gaze in wonder at the treasures of this subtropical wonderland, and they never leave disappointed.

UNDERWATER DENIZENS
A flamingo-tongue cowrie perches on a brilliant violet sea fan, above. Of several species of sponge-eating angelfish to be found in the waters of Biscayne National Park, the French angelfish, below, is perhaps the most spectacular.

a particular shape—such as a staghorn or a huge boulder, in the case of star corals—isn't fully understood, but the mystery of their formation only adds to their allure.

Biscayne National Park contains all the necessary natural elements for the formation of a coral reef: bright sunshine and warm, clear water with just the right amount of salinity. Such reefs are found in the world's warm ocean currents in a 3,000-mile-wide tropical belt around the equator. Since these currents travel in a clockwise direction in the Northern Hemisphere, reef systems are found only along the east coasts of countries north of the equator. (This explains why reefs are absent along Florida's Gulf coast.)

The hard limestone exterior of a coral reef is built on a giant graveyard of countless generations of

NEARBY SITES & ATTRACTIONS

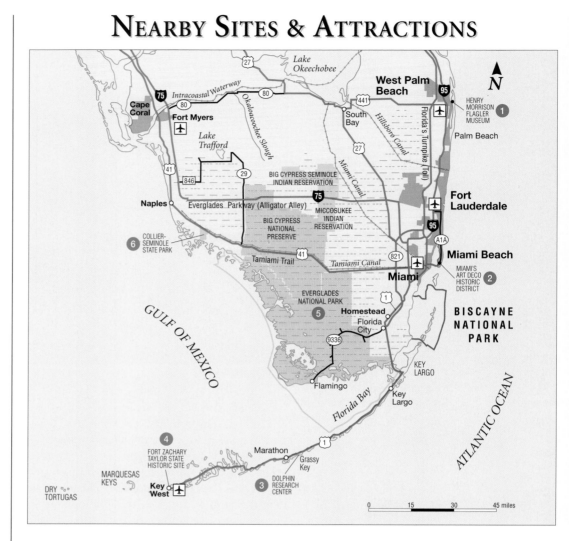

The Henry Morrison Flagler Museum, a magnificent mansion that Flagler built for his wife, Mary Lily Keenan, was opened to the public in 1960. Shown below is the sumptuously appointed Francis I Dining Room.

1 HENRY MORRISON FLAGLER MUSEUM

Oil millionaire Henry Morrison Flagler built the Florida East Coast Railroad and developed many of Florida's resort areas, including St. Augustine, Daytona, Palm Beach, and Miami. Flagler's opulent 55-room estate in Palm Beach, now the site of the Henry Morrison Flagler Museum, was constructed at the turn of the century at a cost of $4 million. Opened to the public in 1960, the lavishly furnished mansion includes Marble Hall, featuring seven different kinds of marble; the guest bedrooms, decorated in different period styles; and the music room, designed to duplicate that of Louis XIV in the Palace of Versailles. There are also displays of porcelain, silver, glass, and dolls, as well as exhibits on local history and Flagler's many enterprises. *The Rambler*, Flagler's personal railroad car, is on the grounds of the estate. Located on Cocoanut Row in Palm Beach.

2 ART DECO HISTORIC DISTRICT

Miami's Art Deco Historic District consists of more than 800 buildings that span more than 80 blocks surrounding Flamingo Park. The sleek-lined, whimsical-hued structures date back to the Miami boom of the 1930's, when developers made extensive use of an architectural style influenced by the 1925 Paris

The spiny softshell turtle thrives in Everglades National Park. Because of its long, sinewy neck, the turtle's nostrils can remain above water while its body lies submerged in a marshy hollow.

Exposition des Arts Décoratifs. Glass-block construction, porthole windows, pipe railings with geometric patterns, and bands of pastel pinks, limes, blues, oranges, and yellows are among the trademark characteristics of the buildings, which were the first structures of the 20th century to be listed on the National Register of Historic Places. Interior adornments include bold murals and etched mirrors of sea nymphs, mermaids, and tropical wildlife. The district stretches from Sixth to Twenty-third Sts. and from Ocean Dr. to Lennox Ct.

③ DOLPHIN RESEARCH CENTER

The Dolphin Research Center houses a colony of dolphins in natural saltwater lagoons, separated from the Gulf of Mexico by only a low fence. Some of the dolphins are born at the center, some arrive from other facilities, and still others have been rescued from distress and restored to health through specialized care. A half-day program for visitors who wish to touch and communicate with these intelligent and sensitive mammals is offered three times a week. Swimming with the dolphins is an especially popular attraction and reservations should be made a month in advance. The center offers special programs for children with learning disabilities. Located on Grassy Key near Marathon.

④ FORT ZACHARY TAYLOR STATE HISTORIC SITE

Fort Zachary Taylor's powerful cannons played an important role in the Civil War, keeping Key West in Union hands while deterring Confederate ships from breaking the Union blockade of the Florida coast. Today the fort's museum boasts the largest collection of Civil War artillery in the entire nation. At the end of the 19th century, the fort's old gun rooms were filled in with armaments and sand in an attempt to shore up the walls. Thanks to the recovery efforts of volunteer workers, six of the 204 original cannons have been unearthed and put on display since 1968. Located in Key West.

⑤ EVERGLADES NATIONAL PARK

On the southern tip of Florida, Everglades National Park's 1.5 million acres of marshes, grasslands, mangrove islands, open waterways, and swamps are the largest remaining subtropical wilderness in the United States. Here crocodiles, alligators, and 800-pound turtles coexist with black bears, Florida panthers, bobcats, otters, and foxes. The park boasts the largest bird community on the continent: it is home to nearly 300 species, from the Florida sandhill crane to the endangered wood stork and roseate spoonbill. A 38-mile-long road traverses the park from Royal Palm to Flamingo; trails include the Anhinga Trail, the Gumbo Limbo Trail, and the Mahogany Hammock Trail, along which visitors can see the largest living mahogany tree in the nation. Located 9 miles west of Homestead on Hwy. 9336.

⑥ COLLIER-SEMINOLE STATE PARK

This 6,423-acre natural preserve in southern Florida bears the name of real estate developer Barron Collier, who donated a portion of the land for the protection of indigenous vegetation and wildlife. The park is also named in honor of the Seminole Indians, who still inhabit the region. Here fresh water mingles with salt water from the Gulf of Mexico to create a unique environment that supports a rich spectrum of plant life. Three distinct vegetation zones are represented within the park's limits: marl prairie, mangrove swamp, and tropical hammock. More than 40 different species of trees alone grow in these zones, including Jamaica dogwood, catclaw, gumbo limbo, strangler fig, royal palm, and four trees from the mangrove family. The park serves as home to a diverse variety of wildlife, including the endangered brown pelican, bald eagle, five-lined skink, indigo snake, and the rare American crocodile. The park is also the habitat of the Florida black bear and the Florida panther—the state's official animal. For a close-up experience of the park's many attractions, visitors can elect to follow a 6.5-mile hiking trail or take a 13.6-mile canoe trip. There are numerous campsites within the park. Located 17 miles south of Naples on Hwy. 41.

A trainer at the Dolphin Research Center tosses food to a hungry Atlantic bottle-nosed dolphin. Committed to the health and welfare of dolphins, the center is a member of the Marine Mammal Stranding Network.

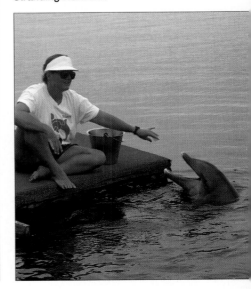

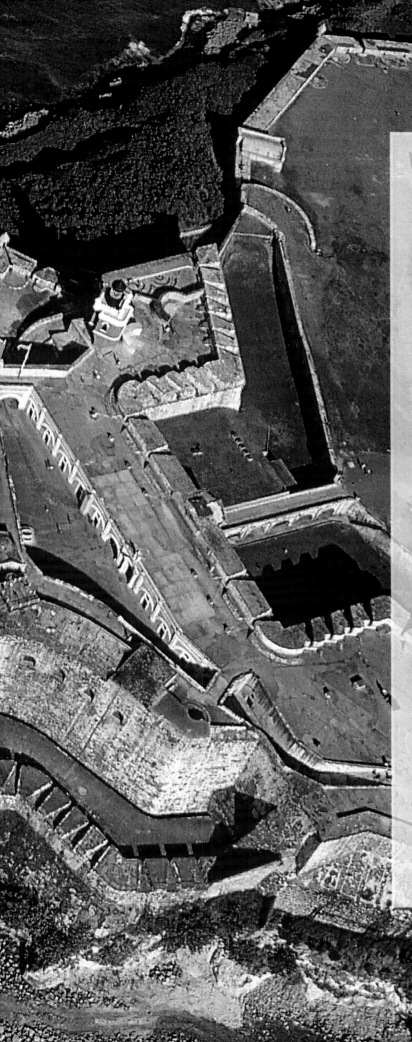

OLD SAN JUAN

The historical landmarks of this tiny corner of Puerto Rico's capital are redolent of its colonial past.

Flanked by the the fortresses of El Morro and San Cristóbal, the seven square blocks of Old San Juan lie sequestered behind city walls up to 20 feet thick and 140 feet high. The flavor of colonial Spain still lingers within this tiny enclave, which is situated on the western tip of an islet that shelters San Juan Bay from the might of Atlantic storms. Its narrow cobbled streets are lined with houses painted in bright pastel hues and filigreed with wrought-iron balconies. Shady plazas and the cool, dark interiors of its many historic churches beckon visitors to step back in time and explore the city's many riches.

Puerto Rico's history stretches back to the 1500's, when Spanish galleons laden with gold and silver from Mexico and South America plied these waters. A deep bay on the north coast of the island became a prized port on the busy sea lanes of the New World. The island was named for its fortuitous location: Puerto Rico means "rich port" in Spanish. Most of the old city is still intact, its varied and striking architecture dating from

Overleaf: An aerial view of El Morro displays the fort's irregular shape. Its location ensured the fort's invincibility from attack by sea.

MOATED MAJESTY

Flanked by towering palm trees and surrounded by gardens, La Fortaleza, below, is distinguished by its palatial architecture.

the 16th century. After falling into disrepair, Old San Juan was rescued in the 1950's by farsighted preservationists and local government agencies working under the guidance of the Institute for Puerto Rican Culture. Today hundreds of privately owned buildings have been restored as homes, shops, galleries, and museums. Dozens more have been renovated into government offices.

As Spain's empire expanded during the 16th century, its European enemies stepped up their attacks on its convoys heading home, laden with treasure from the New World. Fearful that privateers would have an ideal port from which to launch their raiding parties if Puerto Rico fell into British or Dutch hands, the Spanish government began building a fort in 1539 that was strategically located on the rugged headland at the western entrance to San Juan Bay.

A pine-bordered road leads to the fort, a sprawling moated labyrinth with limestone walls 18 feet thick and 140 feet high. Crenellated ramparts give it the look of a medieval castle. The fort, whose full name is Castillo de San Felipe del Morro, is commonly known as El Morro. A stalwart symbol of the Spanish empire, El Morro has withstood five major sieges and the ravages of nature for more than four centuries. The massive redoubt is now

administered by the National Park Service. Visitors can tour the fort's military museum and peer into sentry boxes, living quarters, and cisterns. A triangular staircase, once used as an emergency exit by the Spaniards, leads to El Morro's formidable gun emplacements. Six tiers of cannons still point out to sea.

El Morro last saw hostilities during the Spanish-American War, when it withstood an artillery barrage by U.S. warships. In 1898, at the end of the war, Spain ceded Puerto Rico to the United States, and the Spanish flag that had once flown proudly over this colonial stronghold was finally lowered.

The port city that grew up along a tidy grid of streets and plazas behind the towering walls has proved to be equally resilient. Today, nearly 500 years later, Old San Juan is still a fascinating, vital community that is a colorful, boisterous mixture of old and new.

HISTORIC TOUR

The compact, lively neighborhood is ideal for walking. Many of the streets in the old quarter are paved with blue *adoquines*, or cobblestones, that are said to have been used originally as ballast in Spanish ships. A statue of Christopher Columbus dominates Plaza

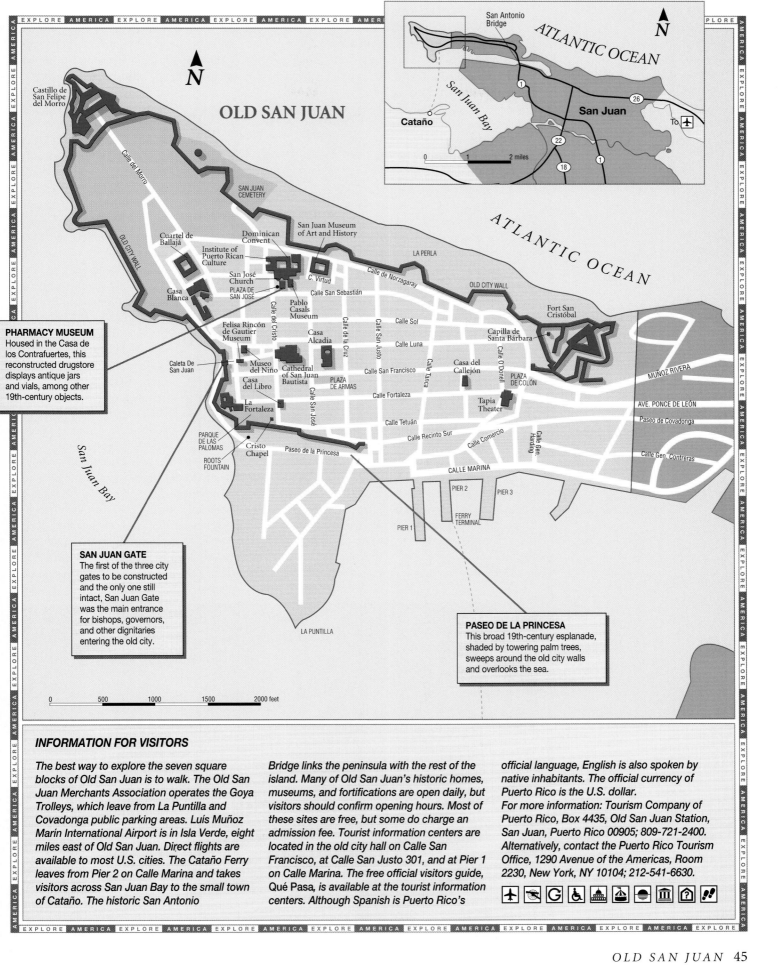

OLD SAN JUAN

ATLANTIC OCEAN

Castillo de San Felipe del Morro

SAN JUAN CEMETERY

Cuartel de Ballajá

Dominican Convent

Institute of Puerto Rican Culture

San Juan Museum of Art and History

LA PERLA

San José Church

C. Virtud

OLD CITY WALL

Casa Blanca

PLAZA DE SAN JOSÉ

Calle San Sebastián

Calle de Norzagaray

Fort San Cristóbal

Pablo Casals Museum

Calle Sol

Calle Luna

Capilla de Santa Bárbara

Felisa Rincón de Gautier Museum

Calle del Cristo

Casa Alcadia

Calle de la Cruz

Calle San Justo

Calle Tanca

Casa del Callejón

Calle O'Donel

PLAZA DE COLÓN

Caleta De San Juan

Museo del Niño

Cathedral of San Juan Bautista

Calle San Francisco

MUÑOZ RIVERA

Casa del Libro

Calle San José

PLAZA DE ARMAS

Calle Fortaleza

Tapia Theater

Calle Gen. Harding

AVE. PONCE DE LEÓN

La Fortaleza

Calle Tetuán

Paseo de Covadonga

PARQUE DE LAS PALOMAS

Calle Recinto Sur

Calle Comercio

Calle Gen. Contreras

Cristo Chapel

Paseo de la Princesa

CALLE MARINA

ROOTS FOUNTAIN

San Juan Bay

PIER 2

PIER 3

FERRY TERMINAL

PIER 1

LA PUNTILLA

ATLANTIC OCEAN

San Antonio Bridge

San Juan Bay

Cataño

San Juan

To ✈

1

26

22

18

1

0   1   2 miles

PHARMACY MUSEUM
Housed in the Casa de los Contrafuertes, this reconstructed drugstore displays antique jars and vials, among other 19th-century objects.

SAN JUAN GATE
The first of the three city gates to be constructed and the only one still intact, San Juan Gate was the main entrance for bishops, governors, and other dignitaries entering the old city.

PASEO DE LA PRINCESA
This broad 19th-century esplanade, shaded by towering palm trees, sweeps around the old city walls and overlooks the sea.

0   500   1000   1500   2000 feet

INFORMATION FOR VISITORS

The best way to explore the seven square blocks of Old San Juan is to walk. The Old San Juan Merchants Association operates the Goya Trolleys, which leave from La Puntilla and Covadonga public parking areas. Luís Muñoz Marín International Airport is in Isla Verde, eight miles east of Old San Juan. Direct flights are available to most U.S. cities. The Cataño Ferry leaves from Pier 2 on Calle Marina and takes visitors across San Juan Bay to the small town of Cataño. The historic San Antonio

Bridge links the peninsula with the rest of the island. Many of Old San Juan's historic homes, museums, and fortifications are open daily, but visitors should confirm opening hours. Most of these sites are free, but some do charge an admission fee. Tourist information centers are located in the old city hall on Calle San Francisco, at Calle San Justo 301, and at Pier 1 on Calle Marina. The free official visitors guide, Qué Pasa, is available at the tourist information centers. Although Spanish is Puerto Rico's

official language, English is also spoken by native inhabitants. The official currency of Puerto Rico is the U.S. dollar.
For more information: Tourism Company of Puerto Rico, Box 4435, Old San Juan Station, San Juan, Puerto Rico 00905; 809-721-2400. Alternatively, contact the Puerto Rico Tourism Office, 1290 Avenue of the Americas, Room 2230, New York, NY 10104; 212-541-6630.

Many of the homes that grace the streets of Old San Juan, opposite page, display the decorative wrought-iron balconies typical of Spanish Colonial architecture.

FANCIFUL FLIGHT

In a refurbished building in the old quarter, the brilliantly colored panels of this stained glass window at right provide the background for a group of birds in flight.

de Colón. When Columbus discovered the island in 1493 on his second voyage to the New World, he named the island San Juan Bautista—St. John the Baptist—for the saint and the royal heir. In the following years, the name of Puerto Rico, which designated the "rich port" on the north coast, came to refer to the entire island, and its principal city was named San Juan.

A stroll west down Calle San Francisco leads to Plaza de Armas—the crossroads of the old city—and once its central marketplace. Four statues, dedicated to the seasons, preside over the plaza. On the north side, Casa Alcadia—the City Hall—dates from 1604 and was restored to its present appearance in 1714. On the plaza's western side, the neoclassical Intendancy Building formerly served as the offices of the royal Spanish Exchequer. Today the building houses Puerto Rico's State Department. Both buildings are open to the public on weekdays.

The Cathedral of San Juan Bautista, with its beautiful stained-glass windows, is located on Calle del Cristo, just west of the Plaza de Armas. Its delightful peach-colored exterior, trimmed in white, dates from the early 19th century. The original structure was built in 1540. The tomb of the colony's founder and first governor, Juan Ponce de León, is located

near the transept. Father Junípero Serra gave a sermon from the pulpit before he set off in the mid-1700's to found a string of missions in California.

A statue of Ponce de León, cast from bronze cannons captured during Sir Ralph Abercromby's abortive attempt to capture San Juan in 1797, stands prominently in Plaza de San José. On the north side of the square, San José Church dates from the 1530's. It is the oldest religious structure in Puerto Rico and the second-oldest in the New World. The remains of Ponce de León reposed in this simple, white-washed house of worship from 1559 to 1908, when they were transferred to the Cathedral of San Juan Bautista. His coat of arms still hangs to the left of the main altar. The cathedral is renowned for its vaulted Gothic ceilings, a feature typical of 16th-century Spanish architecture, and contains a collection of religious paintings.

The nearby cloister of El Convento Dominicano on Calle de Norzagaray was built in 1523 on land that was donated by Ponce de León. The convent, one of Old San Juan's most historic buildings, contains a restored monastic library and chapel. Concerts are sometimes held in the shady, paved courtyard, which is surrounded by two tiers of arcaded galleries lined with richly carved wooden

PORT OF CALL

Cruise ships make regular stops in Puerto Rico, at right, allowing passengers to explore the streets of Old San Juan.

railings. On display in the chapel are music sheets, as well as the altarpiece of St. Thomas Aquinas. Woven crafts, carnival masks, and *santos* (carved and painted wooden religious figures) are sold in the Centro de Artes Populares on the ground floor of the convent.

| MUSEUM RICHES | The Pablo Casals Museum, housed in a handsome two-story building on Plaza de San José, is devoted to one of |

Spain's most prominent cellists. Casals made his home in Puerto Rico in 1957 and soon founded the Casals Festival, an annual June event that brings some of the world's finest musicians to the island. The museum displays some of the great musician's

GOVERNOR'S QUARTERS
The grand interior of La Fortaleza, above, provides a fitting setting for the governor of Puerto Rico. Visitors can tour the mansion, as well as its lavish gardens.

favorite cellos, as well as photographs and memorabilia. The cool, inviting rooms are often filled with the sounds of the maestro's recordings.

The street of Caleta de San Juan is lined with brightly painted town houses. One mansion now houses the Felisa Rincón de Gautier Museum, named in honor of the first woman to serve as the mayor of San Juan, from 1946 to 1968. The Casa del Libro contains the first Spanish Bible, printed in 1559, as well as other illuminated Bibles, one page from a Gutenberg Bible, and an interesting manuscript describing Christopher Columbus' second voyage to the Americas.

At the foot of Calle del Cristo, Cristo Chapel commemorates a reputedly miraculous event that occurred on June 24, 1753—the feast day of San

Juan. During a horse race, a young rider and his horse plunged over the city wall to the rocks below. The rider survived; the fate of the horse goes unrecorded. The rider's safe landing so impressed a bystander that he built a chapel on the site—a simple, cut-stone structure crowned with twin rooftop turrets and a tiny belfry. The white-walled interior is crowded with thousands of so-called *milagros*, or miracles—small silver cutouts in the shapes of legs and arms. Worshipers still hang these charms to give thanks for divine intervention in healing the ailments of their loved ones.

At the end of Calle Fortaleza stands La Fortaleza, also known as the Santa Catalina Palace. Built in 1533 as a fort, the stucture became a government building when El Morro was completed. La Fortaleza is the oldest governor's mansion in the Western Hemisphere: it was occupied for 250 years before the cornerstone was laid for the White House in Washington and it is still in use today. The original single tower and patio were embellished with palatial additions in the 1800's. Guided tours take visitors through the public areas, including the ornate Hall of Mirrors, the informal dining room, the Santa Catalina chapel, the dungeon, and the Blue Room, where formal receptions are held.

| PONCE'S LEGACY | On Columbus' second voyage to the New World, there was a soldier named Juan Ponce de León. He eventually took up |

residence in Santo Domingo, and in 1508 he was given the task of colonizing neighboring Puerto Rico. Named governor the following year, Ponce de León oversaw the colony's difficult first years. In 1512, lured by stories of a fountain with miraculous restorative powers, he embarked on a voyage that would culminate in the discovery of Florida. On a subsequent voyage to Florida in 1521, Ponce de León was mortally wounded and died in Havana, Cuba. Thirty-eight years later his mortal remains were brought back to Puerto Rico.

Two years after Ponce de León left the island, his family began construction of a stone house, which would become the finest dwelling in town. Casa Blanca is an airy, whitewashed villa with lush, fountain-splashed gardens, cool courtyards, and a majestic view of San Juan Bay. The house is now home to two museums. The first one gives visitors a taste of what life was like for the wealthy in the 16th and 17th centuries: the living quarters feature floor-to-ceiling doors, tile floors, and a throne room with two 16th-century Moorish-style armchairs on a raised platform. The second museum is dedicated to the island's Taino Indians, who were wiped out within only 20 years of Ponce de León's arrival on these shores.

ON THE PLAZA
Plaza de Colón, left, is a popular meeting place for local residents. Originally named Plaza de Santiago, the square was renamed in 1893 to honor the 400th anniversary of Columbus' discovery of the island. A statue of the explorer, below, dominates the plaza.

Just north of Casa Blanca looms the green-and-peach-colored Cuartel de Ballajá, the largest military barracks built by Spain in the New World. Completed in 1863 and restored in time for the 500th anniversary of Columbus' arrival in America, the barracks now houses the Museum of the Americas, which presents a comprehensive view of the New World based on folk-art exhibits. A smaller building, originally known as La Beneficiencia, once served as an asylum for the homeless and the infirm. It now houses the Institute of Puerto Rican Culture, which displays prints by international artists.

Fort San Cristóbal dominates the eastern approach to the old city. Attacks on San Juan by Sir Francis Drake in 1595, the third Earl of Cumberland in 1598, and the Dutch in 1625 convinced Spain that stronger fortifications were required to protect the city from land-based attack. In 1635 construction began on the fort and the massive stone walls that encircle the old city. The ramparts on the southern and eastern sides of Old San Juan were demolished in 1895, but the walls still stand on the northern and eastern sides, as does Fort San Cristóbal, which is built entirely from local stone.

The fort is an impressive example of European defense construction of its time. A small yellow chapel—the Capilla de Santa Barbara, patron saint of artillerymen—dominates the center of the courtyard. Scale models of Christopher Columbus' three ships—the *Niña,* the *Pinta,* and the *Santa María*—are on display in the restored barracks.

Although Puerto Rico never yielded the vast quantities of gold and silver that other Spanish colonies poured into Spain's coffers, Old San Juan is still replete with the wealth that was borne of its historical heritage. A strategic stronghold originally designed to fend off outsiders, the tiny hamlet is still a valiant survivor of a once-mighty empire.

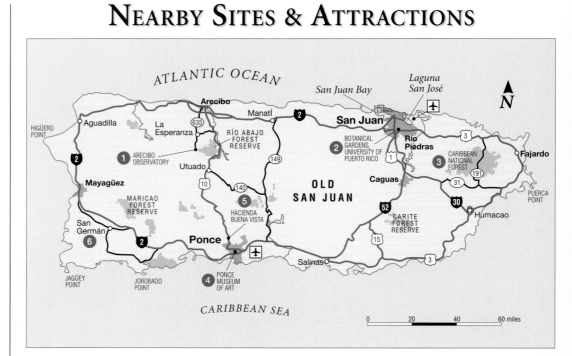

The elegantly furnished dining room of Hacienda Buena Vista provides visitors with a glimpse of a 19th-century plantation home.

1 ARECIBO OBSERVATORY

Built in 1960 and jointly operated by the National Science Foundation and Cornell University, the Arecibo Observatory is the largest radar/radio telescope in the world. Scientists at the observatory monitor radio emissions from distant galaxies, pulsars, and quasars. The observatory dish, suspended over a huge natural sinkhole, is 1,000 feet in diameter and covers an area of 20 acres. The dish is made of nearly 40,000 perforated aluminum mesh panels, each measuring 3 feet by 6 feet. The telescope is so sensitive that it can detect objects 13 billion light years away. Puerto Rico's geographic position—at 17 degrees north of the equator—makes it an ideal location for planetary observations. A viewing platform allows visitors to see the telescope at close range. A 120-seat auditorium and scientific museum provide information about the observatory and its work. Located 21 miles from Arecibo on Hwy. 635.

2 BOTANICAL GARDENS, UNIVERSITY OF PUERTO RICO

Hundreds of species of tropical and subtropical vegetation flourish within these gardens, where many of the flowers along the pathways are identified with labels. Featuring thousands of varieties, the orchid garden is a special highlight. Among the gardens' collections of bamboo plants is one variety that can grow four feet in one day. Water lilies and Egyptian papyrus flourish in the ponds and waterways; cinnamon and nutmeg trees, as well as numerous exotic fruit trees, offer shady spots for picnics. Serious naturalists should contact the Garden Administration in advance in order to see the 36,000 plants in the Herbarium. The gardens are open daily; admission is free. Located at the junction of Hwys. 1 and 847 in Río Piedras.

3 CARIBBEAN NATIONAL FOREST

Originally decreed a protected area by the Spanish in 1876, this 27,846-acre preserve is the only tropical forest within the U.S. National Forest system. The four distinct forest types here are home to more than 245 species of tropical trees, 20 kinds of orchids, and 150 varieties of ferns. The tiny tree frogs inhabiting the forest emit a distinctive cry that has earned them the name "coquis." El Yunque Recreation Area, located in the heart of the forest, is the domain of towering palm trees, as well as the endangered Puerto Rican parrot. El Yunque Trail takes in three of the area's most scenic lookouts; Big Tree Trail leads to a spectacular waterfall known as La Mina. El Toro Trail passes through four levels of rain forest in its climb to the 3,532-foot summit of mighty Pico El Yunque—the highest peak in the forest. Located 35 miles east of San Juan on Hwy. 191.

4 PONCE MUSEUM OF ART

Designed by internationally known architect Edward Durrell Stone, this impressive block-long structure is in itself a work of art that makes use of natural light to illuminate its hexagonal-shaped galleries. The Ponce Museum boasts the finest collections of European and Latin American art in the Caribbean region, with more than 300 works from its collections on permanent display. Of particular interest are works from the museum's prized 19th-century pre-Raphaelite and Italian Baroque collections. Paintings by Murillo, Constable, Gainsborough, and Rubens are among those on exhibit, as are works by acclaimed Puerto Rican masters José Campeche and Francisco Oller. The works of contemporary Puerto Rican and Latin American artists are often featured in temporary exhibitions. Located on Avenida de las Americas in the city of Ponce.

Surrounded by luxuriant foliage, a waterfall tumbles into a natural pool in El Yunque Recreation Area of the Caribbean National Forest. More than 100 billion gallons of annual rainfall sustains this tropical forest.

⑤ HACIENDA BUENA VISTA

This coffee, corn, and citrus plantation was developed by Salvador de Vives, a Spaniard who came to Puerto Rico in 1833. Set amid a subtropical forest along the Canás River, the 19th-century plantation and grain mill have been restored through the efforts of Puerto Rico's Conservation Trust. Today visitors can explore the flour mills and view displays of antique farming artifacts. There are also demonstrations of coffee and grain processing that utilize authentic hydraulic turbines and watermills. The ground floor of the hacienda is now a museum housing old maps, photographs, bills of sale, and other mementos of planter life. Other rooms in the hacienda are furnished with authentic period pieces from the 1850's. Located north of Ponce on Hwy. 10.

⑥ SAN GERMAN

The second-oldest town in Puerto Rico, San Germán was founded in 1573 and has retained a considerable amount of its colonial charm. Two rectangular plazas in the center of town are separated by the city hall, which once served as a prison. Located on the Plaza de los Próceres, Porta Coeli—Latin for "heaven's gate"—is one of the oldest Catholic shrines in the Western Hemisphere. Today it houses a small religious museum with exhibits ranging from a 17th-century portrait of St. Nicholas de Bari to lovely 18th- and 19th-century statues of a black Madonna and Child. The carved main altar's niches are adorned with small wooden statues carved by Puerto Rican, Spanish, Colombian, and Mexican artists. Catedral de San Germán de Auxerre was built in 1739 to honor the town's French patron saint. The Museo de Arte y Casa de Estudio exhibits modern and classic paintings by local artists. Located about 80 miles west of Ponce off Hwy. 2.

The airy galleries of the Ponce Museum of Art showcase Puerto Rico's premier art collection.

St. John

Reborn as a national park, the smallest of the U.S. Virgin Islands abounds with sheer natural beauty.

Floating on the Caribbean Sea like a serpent in slumber, its humpbacked torso cloaked in shades of green, St. John casts a primordial image on the horizon. Its lush hills spill down to deep, secluded bays fringed by snow-white crescents of sand. Offshore, coral reefs teeming with marine life protect the island's shoreline from the whims of the sea. Farther along the coast, mangrove forests provide a haven for many varieties of animals, birds, and plants above and below the surface. Inland, the subtropical forests that cloak St. John's volcanic peaks give way in the southeast to dry cactus-covered cliffs and salt ponds.

A serendipitous past has helped this Caribbean island age with grace. Laurance S. Rockefeller first set foot on St. John at Caneel Bay in 1952. On a six-year odyssey of the Caribbean by yacht, the American philanthropist had dropped anchor at many a winsome isle along the way. But St. John, with its dazzling white beaches and verdant slopes, apparently left the most lasting impression on him. Rockefeller remarked that St. John harbored "the most superb beaches and view" he had ever seen and proceeded to purchase a large portion of

JUNIOR REGATTA
The shallow waters around St. John, above, are popular with recreational boaters young and old.

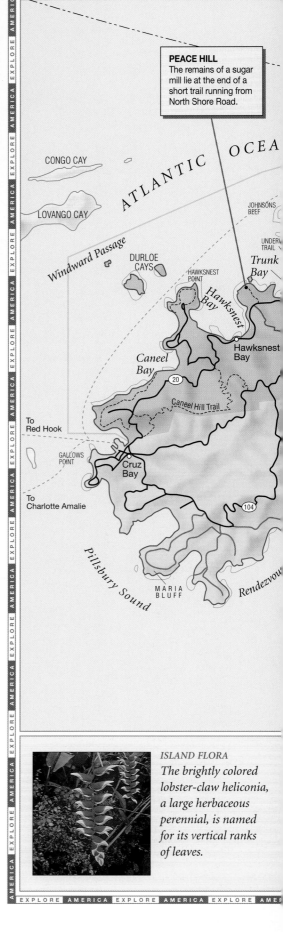

PEACE HILL
The remains of a sugar mill lie at the end of a short trail running from North Shore Road.

CONGO CAY

LOVANGO CAY

ATLANTIC OCEA

JOHNSONS REEF

UNDERW TRAIL

Windward Passage

DURLOE CAYS

HAWKSNEST POINT

Trunk Bay

Hawksnest Bay

Caneel Bay

Hawksnest Bay

20

Caneel Hill Trail

To Red Hook

GALLOWS POINT

Cruz Bay

To Charlotte Amalie

104

Pillsbury Sound

MARIA BLUFF

Rendezvou

ISLAND FLORA
The brightly colored lobster-claw heliconia, a large herbaceous perennial, is named for its vertical ranks of leaves.

the island. He donated most of his holdings—some 5,000 acres in total—to the United States government in 1956 to create a national park. In 1962 the government transferred a further 5,560 acres of submerged lands to the National Park Service, formally establishing the park. Today Virgin Islands National Park comprises slightly more than half of the island.

Placid St. John lies three miles west of populous and developed St. Thomas. Together with St. Croix, roughly 40 miles to the south, these islands make up the most significant portion of the 50 U.S. Virgin Islands, some of which are little more than rocks. To the northeast lie the British Virgins, an archipelago of 50 islands, two of which, Tortola and Virgin Gorda, house most of the population.

COLONIAL TIMES

The vision of St. John as first seen by Old World navigators five centuries ago was probably not much different from that glimpsed by Laurance Rockefeller from his yacht. Christopher Columbus sailed through these waters during his second voyage to the Americas in 1493. Astounded by the sheer number of islands and cays that he encountered, as well as by their natural beauty, he named them after St. Ursula and her legendary 11,000 virgins. Spanish explorers who followed Columbus christened St. John after the apostle of the same name.

Long before the European invasion, two Indian tribes made their homes on St. John. The peace-loving Arawaks farmed its rich soil for a thousand years before the fierce Caribs attacked and conquered them. The Caribs had already left St. John by the time Spanish conquistadors landed on its shores, eager to fill their ships with riches from the New World. The Spaniards found little of value in

CACTUS COUNTRY
Overleaf: Several species of cactus thrive in the dry southeastern part of St. John, such as these Turk's-cap cacti on Ram Head.

54

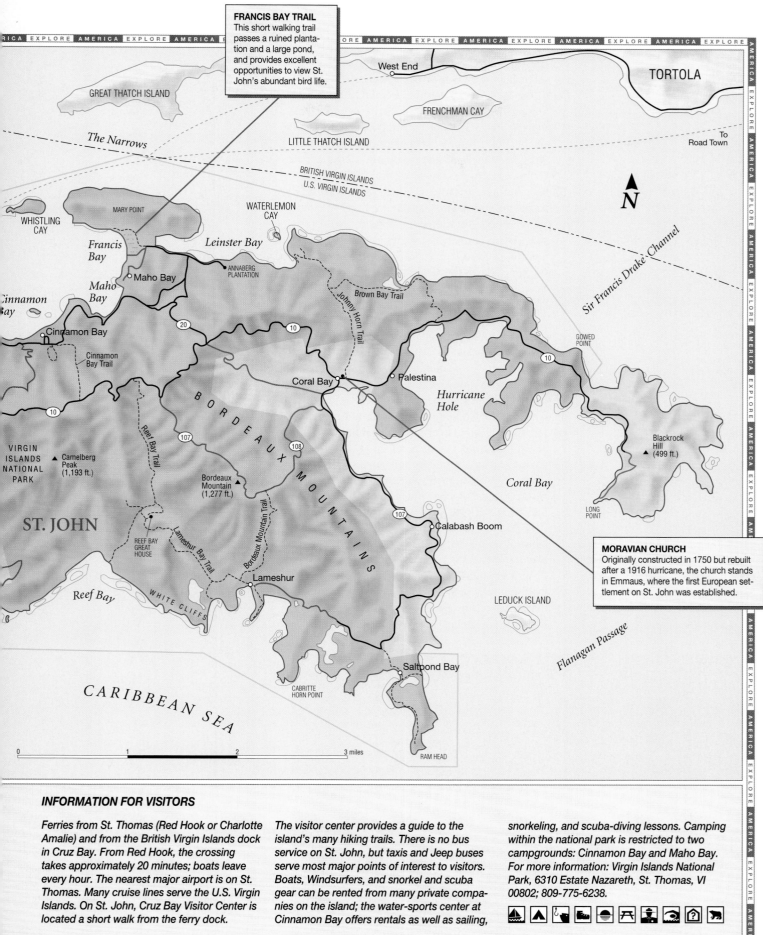

FRANCIS BAY TRAIL
This short walking trail passes a ruined plantation and a large pond, and provides excellent opportunities to view St. John's abundant bird life.

TORTOLA

West End

GREAT THATCH ISLAND

FRENCHMAN CAY

The Narrows

To Road Town

LITTLE THATCH ISLAND

BRITISH VIRGIN ISLANDS
U.S. VIRGIN ISLANDS

WATERLEMON CAY

WHISTLING CAY

MARY POINT

N

Francis Bay

Leinster Bay

ANNABERG PLANTATION

Sir Francis Drake Channel

Maho Bay

Maho Bay

Cinnamon Bay

Brown Bay Trail

Johnny Horn Trail

GOWED POINT

Cinnamon Bay

20

10

Cinnamon Bay Trail

Coral Bay

Palestina

Hurricane Hole

10

10

Reef Bay Trail

107

108

Blackrock Hill (499 ft.)

VIRGIN ISLANDS NATIONAL PARK

▲ Camelberg Peak (1,193 ft.)

Bordeaux Mountain (1,277 ft.) ▲

Coral Bay

ST. JOHN

Lameshur Bay Trail

Bordeaux Mountain Trail

107

REEF BAY GREAT HOUSE

Calabash Boom

LONG POINT

Lameshur

MORAVIAN CHURCH
Originally constructed in 1750 but rebuilt after a 1916 hurricane, the church stands in Emmaus, where the first European settlement on St. John was established.

Reef Bay

WHITE CLIFFS

LEDUCK ISLAND

Flanagan Passage

CABRITTE HORN POINT

Saltpond Bay

CARIBBEAN SEA

RAM HEAD

0   1   2   3 miles

INFORMATION FOR VISITORS

Ferries from St. Thomas (Red Hook or Charlotte Amalie) and from the British Virgin Islands dock in Cruz Bay. From Red Hook, the crossing takes approximately 20 minutes; boats leave every hour. The nearest major airport is on St. Thomas. Many cruise lines serve the U.S. Virgin Islands. On St. John, Cruz Bay Visitor Center is located a short walk from the ferry dock.

The visitor center provides a guide to the island's many hiking trails. There is no bus service on St. John, but taxis and Jeep buses serve most major points of interest to visitors. Boats, Windsurfers, and snorkel and scuba gear can be rented from many private companies on the island; the water-sports center at Cinnamon Bay offers rentals as well as sailing,

snorkeling, and scuba-diving lessons. Camping within the national park is restricted to two campgrounds: Cinnamon Bay and Maho Bay. For more information: Virgin Islands National Park, 6310 Estate Nazareth, St. Thomas, VI 00802; 809-775-6238.

the Virgin Islands, however, and moved on to plunder mineral-rich Hispaniola and Mexico.

During the 17th and 18th centuries, the islands of the West Indies were traded like chess pieces among the European powers. St. John entered the maelstrom in 1717 when the Danish, who had established a colony on St. Thomas, three miles away, formally took possession of the island. The Danes ran a brisk slave trade on St. Thomas and kept enough African slaves there to cultivate their sugarcane and cotton plantations. Eager to establish similar plantations on St. John, the Danish West India and Guinea Company dispatched a handful of Danish and Dutch settlers and a contingent of slaves to the island in 1717.

ISLAND GATEWAY

St. John's first plantation was established at Estate Carolina, near an admirable natural harbor at its eastern end called Coral Bay. The settlement was named for the Danish word *krawl*, or corral, because the settlers started cattle farms there. The moniker was later corrupted to Coral Bay. British naval hero Adm. Horatio Nelson marveled that Coral Bay was large enough to hold the ships of most of Europe's navies. Anticipating a bright future as the island's plantations began to prosper, islanders speculated that traffic in Coral Bay might someday match the bustle of Charlotte Amalie on St. Thomas.

The settlers' prosperity was achieved through the labor of their slaves, who were forced to endure brutal treatment at the hands of their masters. In 1733 a repressive proclamation issued by the Danish governor was one of a number of factors that triggered a savage slave uprising, forcing white settlers to seek refuge on St. John as their cane fields

OFFSHORE INHABITANT
A green sea turtle, below, enjoys a swim in waters near the shore of the island. From June to October, some adult females nest on the beaches of Virgin Islands National Park.

went up in flames. Six months later French troops from Martinique succeeded in restoring order. Local legend has it that hundreds of slaves leaped to their death from the cliffs of Mary Point near Francis Bay rather than submit to European rule. By 1739 St. John's sugar-based economy was flourishing once again.

But prosperity was to be short-lived: in 1848 Denmark abolished slavery. The loss of free labor,

BEGUILING BAY
Cinnamon Bay, at left, boasts one
of St. John's finest natural settings.
Cinnamon Cay, in the middle of
the bay, offers some of the island's
best snorkeling.

together with the advent of the sugar beet, pushed St. John's economy into total collapse. Settlers and freed slaves abandoned the island by the hundreds. St. John's population dwindled from 2,475 in 1835 to 941 in 1911. The remaining islanders survived on subsistence farming and fishing.

St. John captured world attention again in 1917, when it was purchased—along with St. Thomas and St. Croix—by the United States to protect America's access to the Panama Canal during World War I. The Danes' price tag of $25 million made the islands the most expensive U.S. government procurement in history.

It was not until after World War II that St. John began to benefit from what is the U.S. Virgin Islands' major source of revenue today: tourism. When Laurance Rockefeller "discovered" the island more than 40 years ago, St. John was home to about

Probably transplanted from South America to St. John by the Arawak Indians, the ceiba (or kapok) tree, at right, is one of the most striking of the island's nonindigenous species. The Arawaks hollowed out the trunk of the tree to build canoes.

Local handicrafts, such as these brightly colored maracas, above, are on display in many of the shops and markets in St. John.

yachtsmen who anchor in the island's secret bays; and a handful of developers committed to conserving the island's natural splendor by making visitors aware of the wonders around them.

A network of two-lane roads snakes across St. John's mountainous interior. Every twist and turn in these roads reveals glimpses of postcard-perfect beaches and the glistening waters of the sea. The island's highest ridge erupts in three peaks, the loftiest of which is 1,277-foot Bordeaux Mountain. Nearby, wayfarers can see for miles across Sir Francis Drake Channel to the neighboring British Virgin Islands to the northeast.

The island of St. John can be easily explored by foot. By meandering along one of the national park's 22 marked trails, hikers can walk for miles through the island's pristine interior without coming across another person. In the northwestern part of the island, the forest brims with mango and soursop trees, orchids, frangipani, and orange-blossomed flamboyants, which were introduced to the island from Madagascar. The delicate yellow ginger thomas—the official flower of the U.S. Virgin Islands—is a familiar sight. In contrast, a hike in the eastern part of the island reveals a drier habitat more suited to Turk's-cap cactus, prickly pear, and orchids. The park is also home to St. John's only native palm tree, called the teyer palm. The leaves of the bay rum tree, which flourishes within this natural sanctuary, were once harvested for the aromatic oil that was used to make the world-famous bay rum cologne. A large grove of bay rum trees can still be seen at Cinnamon Bay.

Traces of the island's plantation days provide haunting reminders of St. John's past. The Reef Bay Trail—a former wagon road—descends from 800 feet above sea level through wet and dry forests at the shore. This is a section of the old Danish road system, built so that sugarcane, indigo, and raw cotton could be transported down from the upland plantations for shipment to the Danish West India and Guinea Company warehouses in St. Thomas. Today a three-hour downhill trek led

800 residents, who lived without electricity or automobiles. After his mammoth purchase of land, Rockefeller built Caneel Bay—St. John's first self-contained resort—on the grounds of an old sugar plantation. Offering seven pristine beaches, the resort very quickly began to lure well-heeled sunseekers to the island.

In time other developers followed Rockefeller's lead. But there is no doubt that his greatest legacy on St. John remains Virgin Islands National Park. Covering some 12,909 acres of this 21-square-mile island, including 5,560 offshore acres, the park ensures that a large part of St. John will be preserved in its natural state for generations to come.

The neighboring island of St. Thomas, home to dozens of resorts, sends a steady stream of visitors by ferry to St. John. The boats pull into the harbor at Cruz Bay, the island's low-keyed capital. After visitors depart on the ferry for St. Thomas, Cruz Bay returns to its customary torpor. The island is home to an eclectic mix of people: naturalists and hikers drawn to the park; former urbanites who shun the overdeveloped islands of the Caribbean;

by National Park Service rangers takes visitors past the remains of two sugar plantations, including the Reef Bay Great House, which is one of the most ambitious estates on the island. The main house is largely intact: a close look reveals the remains of the cookhouse, servants' quarters, stables, and outhouse of St. John's last working plantation. Along the trail, petroglyphs probably etched by the island's early Indian inhabitants are clearly visible.

Annaberg Plantation on Leinster Bay is another remnant from the past. One of 25 former sugar-producing factories on St. John, Annaberg was built about 1780 and stood amid vast fields of cane. The estate included a small village, slave quarters, a windmill, and a factory where crushed cane was boiled into molasses and then fermented and distilled into rum. The ruins of many of these structures are still standing.

THE LAND RENEWED

European settlers cleared much of St. John's forest to make way for plantations, as well as to produce charcoal. Settlers also introduced many foreign plants and shrubs, including wild tamarind and genip. Since the early 1900's, the forest has staged a comeback.

Despite its wealth in plant species (more than 800 at last count), St. John is home to relatively

PLANTATION DAYS
The ruins of the Annaberg Plantation, below, are a reminder that the island once had thriving sugar and cotton industries. Built of coral blocks and bricks brought over as ballast in Danish ships, the buildings on the Annaberg estate were partially reconstructed during the 1960's and today are a popular attraction for those seeking to learn more about the island's history.

With the blue waters of the Caribbean beckoningly within reach, a beach hammock near Gallows Point, below, offers a laid-back approach to enjoying St. John's natural charms.

few members of the animal kingdom. Even so, more than 20 species of tropical birds come to the island to breed. Lizards bolt across trails at lightning speed, and occasionally visitors spot one of the diminutive white-tailed deer that inhabit wooded areas. St. John's only native mammal is the bat, but observant hikers may notice the ferretlike mongoose that darts through the woods. Introduced by European settlers in order to control the rat population, the mongoose now preys upon the island's lizards and devours the eggs of the endan-

gered hawksbill and green sea turtles. The mongoose is mainly active during the day, so it seldom crosses paths with the nocturnal rat population.

The ultimate reward after a hike is to wind up on one of the island's many pristine beaches. Inviting bays with names such as Caneel, Hawksnest, Trunk, Cinnamon, and Maho dot the north shore of the island like a strand of pearls, each one more lustrous than the last. After resting on the talcum sand in the shade of palm and sea-grape trees to watch brown pelicans dive-bomb

for prey, visitors may feel drawn to explore St. John's brilliant underwater world. Although the self-guided snorkeling trail at Trunk Bay is showing signs of wear and tear, colorful fish can still be seen at many other underwater spots that reveal an abundance of reef life. At Waterlemon Cay, a tiny islet off Leinster Bay, coral, tube sponges, and gorgonians such as sea whips and sea fans provide a vivid backdrop to a parade of sea creatures that include parrotfish, peacock flounders, trunk fish, and sergeant majors. Dramatic southern stingrays

and eagle rays skim over the sea floor, while sea turtles swim playfully over coral canyons.

Red mangrove trees line the waters along sheltered stretches of shoreline. Easily identified by their exposed proplike root system, mangroves play an important part in the chain of life that exists on the island. Their dense roots protect a diverse web of life, ranging from algae, anemones, barnacles and oysters to juvenile groupers, barracudas, doctorfish, sardines, and snappers.

Despite the crowds that cluster in Cruz Bay and along the beaches nearby, an escapist can still find a deserted beach, a secluded cove, or an empty trail on St. John. To stare a hawksbill or green turtle in the eye, to stumble upon a centuries-old mahogany tree, or to kayak along a rocky shore with hundreds of brown boobies is to discover the lure of a gentle island where nature is here to stay.

LATE BLOOMER
The century plant, above, is commonly seen in St. John's arid regions. The plant grows for about 20 years, sends up a 10- to 20-foot yellow flowering stalk, and then dies. The plant attracts a number of bird species, such as the pearly-eyed thrasher.

SUNNING SESSION
Sharp-eyed visitors may spot a dinosaurlike iguana, left, basking in the tropical sun. Although now a rare sight in St. John, the iguana is a very common creature on the sister island of St. Thomas.

Nearby Sites & Attractions

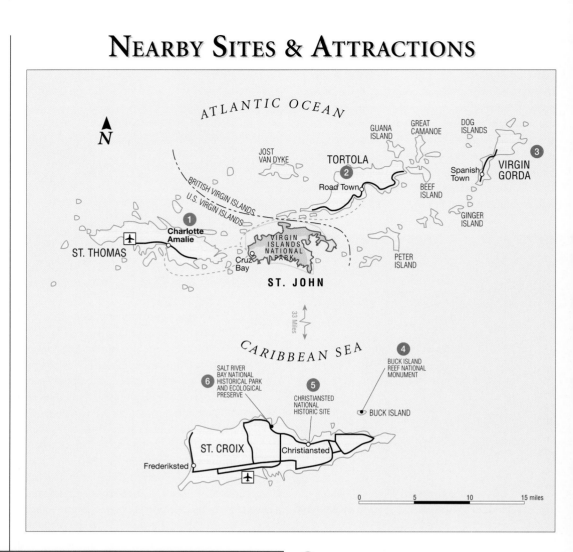

Many of the inviting beaches along Virgin Gorda's southwestern coast are dotted with granite boulders spewed up by the volcanic activity that created the island.

① CHARLOTTE AMALIE, ST. THOMAS

Settled in 1691 and named for Danish queen Charlotte Amalie, the picturesque capital city of the U.S. Virgin Islands exudes European charm and is a popular stop for Caribbean cruise ships. White and pastel-painted houses cling to the towering green hills surrounding the city. Government House, the official residence of the governor, and the Legislature Building, home of the Virgin Islands Senate, are outstanding examples of 19th-century Danish Colonial architecture. Both these buildings are open to the public. The second-oldest synagogue in the Americas, the Congregation of Blessing, Peace, and Loving Deeds, was built here in 1833. The sand-floored sanctuary houses a menorah from Spain that dates back to the 11th century, as well as a rare Torah scroll that was rescued from the Holocaust. Emancipation Garden is dedicated to the slaves freed on the island in 1848. Located on Hwy. 30.

② TORTOLA, BRITISH VIRGIN ISLANDS

The largest and most populated of the British Virgin Islands, Tortola has varied terrain ranging from inland mountains to long stretches of white sandy beaches. Gravel pathways allow visitors to explore the lush vegetation of Sage Mountain National Park. Giant elephant ear philodendrons, lacy ferns, palicourea, and cocoplum plants thrive within this tropical environment. The park is dominated by 1,780-foot-high Sage Mountain, the highest point on the island. The capital city, Road Town, contains sites of natural beauty and historic importance. The J. R. O'Neal Botanic Gardens display many species of indigenous and exotic tropical plants, including frangipani and ginger. The V. I. Folk Museum exhibits artifacts of the island's earliest inhabitants, the Taino Indians. Tortola is also popular with swimming, snorkeling, scuba-diving, sailing, and fishing enthusiasts. Located 2 miles northeast of St. John.

3 VIRGIN GORDA, BRITISH VIRGIN ISLANDS

Second largest of the British Virgin Islands, Virgin Gorda has been preserved in its pristine beauty within the island's many national parks. Large granite boulders, located along the seaside, form a chain of small grottos and pools in The Baths National Park, where the calm waters between the boulders are ideal for snorkeling and swimming. Overland and coastal trails link the park with Devil's Bay National Park, which boasts a colorful coral sand beach. Gorda Peak National Park preserves the largest virgin stands of forest on all of the islands, including mahogany trees, and is topped by 1,359-foot-high Gorda Peak. Many different species of indigenous and exotic plants, birds, and animals inhabit the park. There are also numerous hiking trails and picnic areas within the parks. Located 14 miles northeast of St. John.

4 BUCK ISLAND REEF NATIONAL MONUMENT

One of the premier spots in the U.S. Caribbean for scuba diving and snorkeling, the reef encircling the eastern two-thirds of Buck Island was formed through the accumulation of the skeletons of tiny creatures known as coral polyps. Buck Island Reef features coral formations named for their distinctive shapes, including staghorn, brain, and elkhorn, which comprise more than 80 percent of the barrier reef. About 300 species of fish, including blue tang, French grunts, trumpetfish, damselfish, and parrotfish, live in and around the reef, which provides protection from predators such as barracudas, tarpons, and groupers. An underwater trail through the coral grotto is one of the monument's most popular attractions. The island's interior contains 175 acres of tropical dry forest; a hiking trail leads to an observation tower located 200 feet above sea level overlooking the north barrier reef. Buck Island provides a habitat for rare native plants and trees, and nesting and foraging areas for endangered hawksbill and leatherback sea turtles, as well as threatened green sea turtles and brown pelicans. Located 1.5 miles north of St. Croix.

5 CHRISTIANSTED NATIONAL HISTORIC SITE, ST. CROIX

When the Danish West India and Guinea Company purchased the island of St. Croix from France in 1733, the company established a fortified settlement, which they called Christiansted. From 1754 to 1871,

Christiansted served as the capital of the Danish West Indies. Christiansted National Historic Site encompasses five buildings located along the waterfront, all dating back to Danish colonial days. The ramparts, dungeons, and cannons of Fort Christiansvaern, which saw active service between 1738 and 1878, are open to the public. The Old Scale House, located nearby, was used by Danish Customs officials to weigh imports and exports for tax purposes. The Steeple Building, originally a Lutheran church, now houses a museum. On exhibit are artifacts from early St. Croix Indian settlements, as well as architecture and black history displays. The courtyard of the West India and Guinea Company Warehouse, constructed in 1749, was once the site of slave auctions. The Danish Customs House, built in 1830, now serves as the site's administrative headquarters. Located in Christiansted on St. Croix.

6 SALT RIVER BAY NATIONAL HISTORICAL PARK AND ECOLOGICAL PRESERVE, ST. CROIX

The preserve marks the site of the first documented clash between Europeans and Native Americans, which occurred on November 14, 1493, when Christopher Columbus and his crew faced the fierce Carib Indians. A plaque on the beach marks the spot where Columbus' men landed on their second voyage to the New World. Native settlement long predated their arrival: there is evidence of an ancient ball court—similar to others found in Central America—that is unique in the Lesser Antilles. The centerpiece of the Salt River Bay ecosystem is the mangrove forest, where red, black, and white mangroves offer a haven for hundreds of species of birds and fish. The preserve is a sanctuary for endangered creatures such as the roseate tern and hawksbill turtle. Offshore, an incredible coral reef system offers superb opportunities for scuba diving. Located on the north shore 5 miles west of Christiansted.

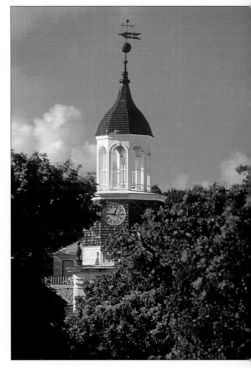

The white spire of the Steeple Building in Christiansted is one of the city's historic landmarks.

The streets of Charlotte Amalie are thronged with dancers in brightly colored clothing during its annual carnival in April. Steel bands and floats add to the festival flavor.

GALVESTON ISLAND

A barrier island often imperiled by wind and sea, Galveston revels in its colorful past.

Approached from the west—from Treasure Isle and the bridge that spans the swift currents of San Luis Pass—Galveston Island appears an unspectacular and uninviting wisp of real estate: part marsh, part prairie, and narrow enough to shout across. Slender weeds and tall grasses bend with the wind on the Galveston Bay side of the road; parched dunes and mud plains slide toward the Gulf of Mexico on the other. With the distant drone of the surf and shorebirds circling silently above the coastline, this end of Galveston Island possesses a desolate, forlorn countenance. Habitation seems preposterous, and even the highway is an intrusion.

Lying across the mouth of Galveston Bay, a mere 50 miles south of Houston, Texas, this 30-mile-long island is just one of the long string of barrier islands that extend south from New York, around Florida, and all the way along the Texas coast to Mexico. Galveston's offshore location makes it a part of Texas, yet sets it uniquely apart from the Lone Star State.

From this vantage point, then, it is not surprising that the first known residents of the island were the Karankawas, a nomadic tribe that roamed the Texas coast 200 to 600 years ago. Some historians believe the Karankawas arrived about A.D. 1400 and spent as much as half of each year on Galveston Island. They practiced ceremonial cannibalism and also feasted on the abundance of game birds, edible roots, and the Gulf's own bounty of clams, oysters, and fish until the mid-1800's. From the time of the Karankawas to the present, Galveston Island has been a place of refuge, whether for Native Americans, pirates, adventurers, smugglers, merchant barons, gamblers, revolutionaries, or the humble immigrants who settled here.

ISLAND ON THE EDGE

Soon after crossing the bridge onto the southwestern end of the island, the sandbar widens to as much as half a mile, and seaside dwellings perched on stilts begin to appear. While they may look eccentric, they are designed to afford protection from a very real threat.

Through the years, hurricanes have visited Galveston Island with deadly regularity. The cataclysm of September 1900, which killed at least 6,000 people, was the worst natural disaster ever to strike North America. But Galveston's residents returned and rebuilt their city. The island's modern residents include those affectionately known as BOI's (Born on Island), who tend to live in the city—now protected by a seawall. West of the Galveston city limits, the island is dotted with vacation and second homes built on stilts to avoid the fury of the Gulf's next assault. The combination of fatalism and defiance of nature shown by its residents

has, perhaps more than anything else, shaped life on Galveston Island from its very beginnings.

Farther along the road that runs the length of the island, palms shoot up from sandy beaches and stands of oaks appear. Here and there, small clusters of cattle graze. Restaurants, shopping centers, campgrounds, wealthy subdivisions on stilts, and the first high-rise condominiums point the way to the city of Galveston, where the flat baldness of the land turns green and subtropical. Spreading oaks and oleanders mingle with the palms to form shady canopies over the boulevards and trolley routes. The neighborhoods are brightened by jasmine and magnolia blossoms, and office spires are visible over the rooftops of aging houses that sit on piers of brick and stone.

Here the island ceases to resemble a sandbar. It widens to two miles or more—a sufficiently large enough land mass to support Galveston's raucous, prosperous, and serendipitous history, as well as its more sedate present.

The first Europeans to set foot on the island were Spanish explorers from the Narvaez expedition who washed ashore in 1528 after their ship was wrecked in a Gulf storm. Among them was Alvar Núñez Cabeza de Vaca, who recounted the castaways' tale—which included capture by the Karankawas—after he and three other survivors made the harrowing overland trek back to Mexico. In 1783 Galveston Bay was surveyed and charted by Spanish navigator José de Evia, who named it the Bay of Gálvez in honor of Bernardo de Gálvez, viceroy of Mexico and former Spanish governor of Louisiana.

Galveston Island soon became the haunt of pirates. In 1816 French privateer Louis-Michel

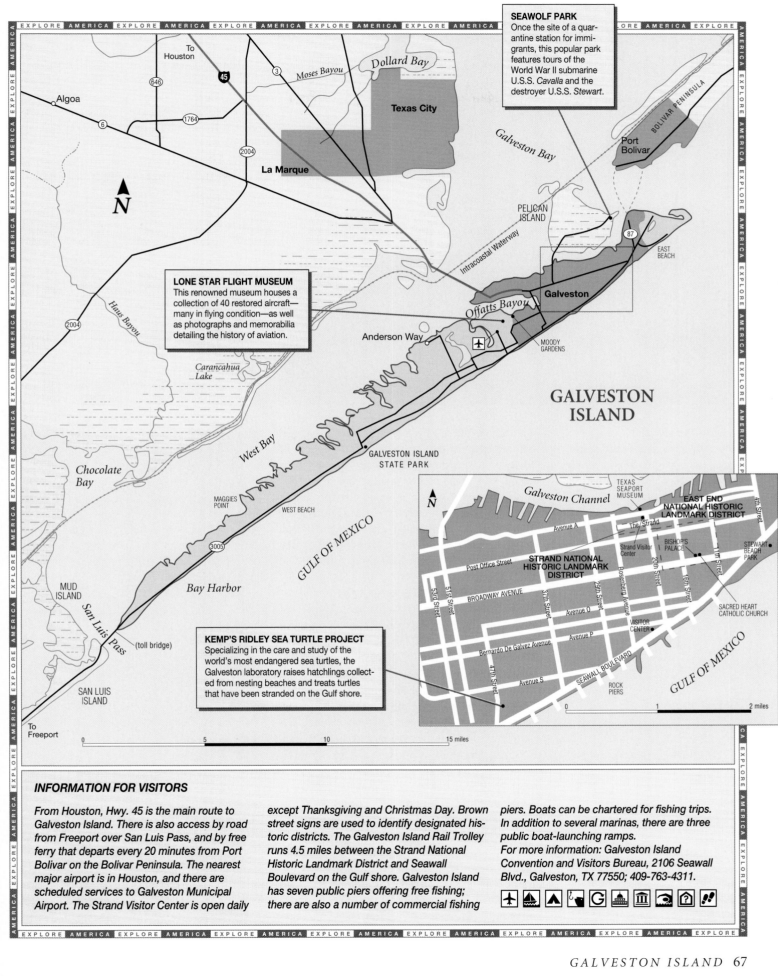

SEAWOLF PARK
Once the site of a quarantine station for immigrants, this popular park features tours of the World War II submarine U.S.S. *Cavalla* and the destroyer U.S.S. *Stewart*.

Dollard Bay

Texas City

To Houston

Algoa

La Marque

Galveston Bay

Moses Bayou

Port Bolivar

BOLIVAR PENINSULA

PELICAN ISLAND

Intracoastal Waterway

EAST BEACH

LONE STAR FLIGHT MUSEUM
This renowned museum houses a collection of 40 restored aircraft—many in flying condition—as well as photographs and memorabilia detailing the history of aviation.

Offatts Bayou

Galveston

Haus Bayou

Anderson Way

MOODY GARDENS

Carancahua Lake

GALVESTON ISLAND

West Bay

GALVESTON ISLAND STATE PARK

Chocolate Bay

MAGGIES POINT

WEST BEACH

GULF OF MEXICO

MUD ISLAND

Bay Harbor

San Luis Pass

(toll bridge)

SAN LUIS ISLAND

To Freeport

KEMP'S RIDLEY SEA TURTLE PROJECT
Specializing in the care and study of the world's most endangered sea turtles, the Galveston laboratory raises hatchlings collected from nesting beaches and treats turtles that have been stranded on the Gulf shore.

0   5   10   15 miles

Galveston Channel

TEXAS SEAPORT MUSEUM

EAST END NATIONAL HISTORIC LANDMARK DISTRICT

Avenue A

The Strand

Strand Visitor Center

BISHOP'S PALACE

STEWART BEACH PARK

STRAND NATIONAL HISTORIC LANDMARK DISTRICT

Post Office Street

BROADWAY AVENUE

Avenue O

Avenue P

Bernardo De Galvez Avenue

Avenue S

VISITOR CENTER

SEAWALL BOULEVARD

ROCK PIERS

SACRED HEART CATHOLIC CHURCH

GULF OF MEXICO

0   1   2 miles

INFORMATION FOR VISITORS

From Houston, Hwy. 45 is the main route to Galveston Island. There is also access by road from Freeport over San Luis Pass, and by free ferry that departs every 20 minutes from Port Bolivar on the Bolivar Peninsula. The nearest major airport is in Houston, and there are scheduled services to Galveston Municipal Airport. The Strand Visitor Center is open daily except Thanksgiving and Christmas Day. Brown street signs are used to identify designated historic districts. The Galveston Island Rail Trolley runs 4.5 miles between the Strand National Historic Landmark District and Seawall Boulevard on the Gulf shore. Galveston Island has seven public piers offering free fishing; there are also a number of commercial fishing piers. Boats can be chartered for fishing trips. In addition to several marinas, there are three public boat-launching ramps.

For more information: Galveston Island Convention and Visitors Bureau, 2106 Seawall Blvd., Galveston, TX 77550; 409-763-4311.

EPISCOPAL MANSE
Although the sumptuous Bishop's Palace now serves as the residence of Galveston's Catholic bishop, the house was built in 1893 for Col. Walter Gresham, a prominent local businessman. In 1956 the American Institute of Architecture designated the house one of the 100 outstanding buildings in the United States.

Gail Borden, a pioneer surveyor, was one of those hired to lay out the city's streets. Mindful of the hardships endured by the pioneers, Borden tried to develop foods that would not spoil quickly on the trail. While living in Galveston, he developed a biscuit made from concentrated meat. But Borden's inventiveness would not bear fruit until his return to New England: in 1856, Borden invented and patented the process for producing condensed milk.

By the mid-1850's grand and ornate edifices had sprung up along the avenues in a riot of architectural styles—Italianate, Greek Revival, Victorian, French Colonial, and Early American. Many withstood the hurricane assaults and survive today as museum pieces or civic gathering places. The city's main commercial area, known as the Strand, is on the bay side of the island, where cobbled streets run between warehouses, office buildings, restaurants, theaters, and an opera house. Because of its wealth of fine architecture, the Strand is sometimes called the Wall Street of the Southwest.

Cotton exports brought immense wealth to the city's merchants and made Galveston into a world-class port. Although placed under Union block-

Aury arrived here with a fleet of 12 to 15 vessels. Although he was chosen by the infant Republic of Mexico as governor of Texas and of Galveston Island, Aury's reign was to be shortlived. In 1817 the pirate Jean Lafitte—renowned for his heroic exploits at the Battle of New Orleans during the War of 1812—established a base on the island, which he called Campeachy. From here, his men preyed on Spanish merchant ships going to and from Mexico.

Between 1817 and 1821, when he left the island at the behest of the U.S. government, Lafitte had built a thriving center of commerce. Within a year of his arrival, Galveston Island boasted a fortress, arsenal, dockyard, many homes, more than 1,000 people, and an active slave market. A hurricane virtually destroyed it all in September 1818, but Lafitte rebuilt his empire and continued to prosper. Ships from New York, Boston, New Orleans, and Europe came to buy or barter for his Spanish loot.

During the 1830's Galveston was occupied by Texas revolutionaries fighting for independence from Mexico. After Texas won independence in 1836, warehouses and docks went up along the channel into Galveston Bay. Merchants, shippers, land speculators, bankers, and publishers flocked to the island and began to build a city. By the 1840's waves of immigrants had begun to arrive from Europe on their way to settle the interior. Although it was prone to hot, wet, and disease-bearing summers and frequently chilly winters, Galveston prospered as the portal to the immense New World.

ade during the Civil War, the city returned to prosperity after the end of hostilities. In 1883 Galveston became the first city in the state of Texas to be lit by electricity. The elegance of its lifestyle, as well as the feverish tempo of its trade seemed incongruous on an island where mere survival was so difficult, but the islanders were able to overcome almost everything that nature could throw at them—snakes, mosquitoes, yellow fever, heat, and cold—except for the angry winds.

DEVASTATION AND REBIRTH

The most belligerent hurricane the island had ever seen arrived on a September weekend in 1900. It swept over the sandbar at more than 120 miles an hour, scattering ships and railroad cars like toys, leveling houses, flooding buildings, shattering windows, collapsing trestles and bridges, and snapping telegraph lines. Mountainous waves washed over the island, completely submerging it. Every building along the shoreline was obliterated, and in some places the beach was moved back nearly a quarter of a mile. It took months to find and dispose of the dead.

But rather than abandon the island, Galveston's residents spent the next two years fortifying it. The county authorities built a seawall more than three miles in length, 16 feet wide, and 16 feet tall. Silt dredged from Galveston Bay was used to raise the city's elevation. As a result, many buildings and residences had to be jacked up to the new level. In 1905 the U.S. Army Corps of Engineers extended the seawall farther to the west. The current seawall, backed with sand and sheathed in granite and sandstone, extends for some 10 miles.

By 1910 virtually the entire city had been rebuilt. While Galveston was recovering from the hurricane, however, Houston had dredged a shipping channel to allow oceangoing vessels to sail into its port. Houston soon became Texas' premier port and Galveston slipped into a slow twilight.

During the next 50 years, however, Galveston acquired the reputation of being a wide-open town, thumbing its nose at the morality and laws of the mainland. Tourists came in droves for the night life as much as for the surf. Along Post Office Street, prostitutes operated with tacit official sanction and gambling houses sprang up on the piers of the city's

A CHRISTMAS CAROL
Dressed for an English winter, these handbell ringers bring a touch of Christmas cheer to Galveston's annual Dickens on the Strand Festival. Since 1973 the city has celebrated its Victorian heritage by honoring the great English writer.

SEAFARING HERITAGE
Galveston is still a working port, as the sturdy shrimp boat in the foreground attests. In the background is the Elissa, a restored three-masted iron bark built in Aberdeen, Scotland, in 1877. The ship forms the centerpiece of Galveston's Texas Seaport Museum.

LONG-LEGGED WADER
Alert for a tasty morsel from the sea, the semipalmated sandpiper, right, is a frequent sight along the Gulf coast of Texas.

PRIMROSE PATH
New life springs from the dunes of Galveston's Gulf coast as primroses spread their yellow blooms, below. The sunlit sea gives little hint of the ferocity with which it has ravaged the island in the past.

waterfront. During Prohibition, bootleg whiskey kept the gin parlors jumping.

The rich, famous, and powerful often came to Galveston. Franklin D. Roosevelt came here to fish. Entertainers like Frank Sinatra, Sophie Tucker, and Bob Hope headlined at local clubs. Band leader Phil Harris and singer Alice Faye were married in the penthouse suite of the Galvez Hotel, which was also the home of Sam Maceo, one of the island's most prominent illegal gamblers. Galveston's free-wheeling ways lasted until the late 1950's, when a crusading state attorney general methodically began to crack down on the vice.

LIVING HISTORY

Today Galveston Island is mainly a tourist destination. After declining to the status of a slum by the early 1960's, Galveston's handsome Victorian warehouses and commercial buildings began to undergo extensive rehabilitation when Galvestonians woke up to the fact that their architectural heritage was in jeopardy. The historic buildings of the Strand were restored and turned into restaurants, emporiums, souvenir shops, art galleries, and taverns. Horse-drawn coaches now ply the streets with visitors rather than cotton bales. The Strand Visitor Center, located in the heart of the Strand National Historic Landmark District, is the first stop for visitors wishing to sample this unique part of the city. Trolleys provide an easy way to tour the city center.

Among the island's main points of interest, none is more spectacular than Moody Gardens, a 156-acre plot where horticulturists maintain 20,000 plants and trees. The centerpiece of the garden is a 40,000-square-foot rain forest enclosed in a 10-story glass pyramid that is home to more than 2,000 species of exotic plants, fish, and butterflies indigenous to Asia, Africa, and South America.

In recent years the beaches along the seawall have been rebuilt with sand dredged from the Gulf of Mexico. On the Galveston Bay side, new shops and restaurants have sprung up near the wharves beside snapper boats, shrimpers, and fish markets.

Galveston pays generous attention to the past. The main thoroughfare—Broadway—is dotted with monuments to the dead of every war since the Texas Revolution. Museums house vintage trains, automobiles, airplanes, and even a tall ship. But the past here also lives on in a gallery of the senses. Fragments of everything the island ever was seem to hang in the Gulf winds like a molecular imprint of long-vanished faces and voices.

"Coming down the coastal prairie from Houston, you can smell the ghosts before you see them," wrote Texas author Gary Cartwright. "They smell sweet and moldy, like the unfocused memory of some lost sensation jarred unexpectedly to mind." For all its attention to its mansions and manicured parks, Galveston has not erased the ghosts and probably does not want to. The 59,000 residents live as comfortably with them as they live with the perils of nature. The two, after all, are inseparable.

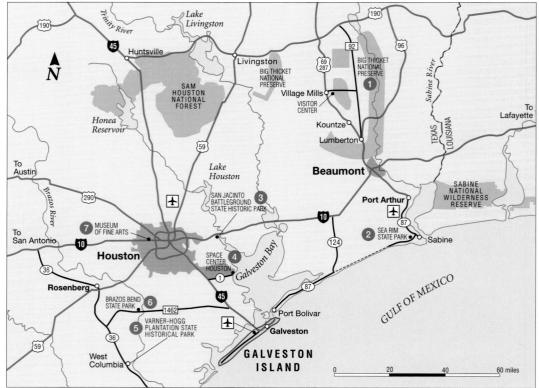

Crowned by a mighty 220-ton Lone Star, the 570-foot San Jacinto Monument stands amid 1,000 acres of parkland. The imposing monument was completed in 1939 as part of the centennial celebration of the decisive battle that won independence for Texas.

① BIG THICKET NATIONAL PRESERVE

The preserve consists of 86,000 acres divided into 12 sections, each a different major biological unit, such as savannah, floodplain forest, flatlands palmetto hardwood, and pine forest. Its incredible wealth of plant and animal species has given Big Thicket the nickname of the "American Ark." This remarkable diversity is attributable to the last ice age, when a great variety of species were pushed south, where they mixed with local species. Today four of North America's five carnivorous plants are found in the preserve, along with 26 different ferns and 85 species of trees. Wood ducks, yellow-billed cuckoos, roadrunners, pileated woodpeckers, and painted buntings are among the 300 different kinds of birds that may be sighted here. There are 50 reptile species, including coral snakes, speckled king snakes, and marbled salamanders. A 74-mile driving tour takes in all 12 units. There are also numerous hiking trails, as well as boat and canoe routes. The visitor center is located 7 miles north of Kountze on Hwy. 69-287.

② SEA RIM STATE PARK

Blessed with sea-swept beaches and tidal marshes, this portion of the Gulf coast was formed when sediment washed down by the Sabine River was swept along the coastal shore by currents. The 5.2-mile stretch of the park's coastline is divided into sandy beaches that are ideal for swimming and an adjoining area where the marshes drain into the ocean. The nutrient-rich marshlands are home to shrimp and crab, and also support a diverse wildlife, including rabbits, opossums, minks, raccoons, skunks, nutria, and river otters. Sea Rim is visited by more than 300 species of birds, particularly during the winter and spring migration periods. Canoe trails afford an ideal opportunity to view the park's wildlife, as does the Gambusia Nature Trail, a boardwalk that winds through the marsh. Located south of Port Arthur on Hwy. 87.

③ SAN JACINTO BATTLEGROUND STATE HISTORIC PARK

A 570-foot monumental column—the tallest in the world—marks the site of the battle of San Jacinto, which paved the way for Texas independence from Mexico. It was here in 1836 that Sam Houston led his Texas revolutionary army to victory over Mexican forces under Antonio López de Santa Anna. An elevator takes visitors 489 feet up the monument for a spectacular panorama of the city of Houston. At the base of the monument, the San Jacinto Museum of History exhibits paintings, manuscripts, and books that document 400 years of Texas history. A multimedia presentation titled "Texas Forever" tells the dramatic story of the state's struggle for independence. Outside the museum, eight stone relief panels immortalize key events of the Texas Revolution. Visitors can also tour the restored battleship *Texas*, moored at the western end of the park since San Jacinto Day in 1948. Commissioned in 1914, the *Texas* is the only surviving American naval ship to have seen service in both world wars. Located 21 miles east of Houston off Hwy. 10.

SPACE CENTER HOUSTON

The exciting drama of space exploration comes vividly to life during a tour of Space Center Houston, which is part of NASA's Johnson Space Center. Here amateur astronauts can take an interactive journey into the past, present, and future of NASA's manned space program. The Space Center's IMAX cinema shows film footage from several shuttle flights. In Space Center Plaza, a mock-up of the space shuttle offers participants a close-up look at the flight deck and allows them to imagine what it would be like to pilot the craft. At the Mission Status Center, visitors can listen to recorded conversations between Mission Control and astronauts aboard the shuttle. Interactive computer simulators permit participants to land the shuttle or retrieve a satellite. Other live demonstrations allow visitors to perform routine activities such as eating, sleeping, and showering as if they were in space. Located in the southwestern corner of Johnson Space Center, 20 miles south of Houston off Hwy. 45.

🅖 ♿ 🏛

5 VARNER-HOGG PLANTATION STATE HISTORICAL PARK

This two-story Colonial Revival plantation mansion boasts a fine collection of Early American and antebellum furniture, antiques, paintings, and assorted family memorabilia collected by Ima Hogg, daughter of former Texas governor James Stephen Hogg. The present house was constructed by Columbus R. Patton in about 1835 to replace a modest log cabin that had been built by the property's first owner, sugar planter Martin Varner. Governor Hogg purchased the house in 1901 for use as a summer residence. Convinced that the land would yield oil, Hogg was only proven right after his death, when the discovery of oil on the property made his family one of the wealthiest in the state. A tour of the house includes the entrance hall, the parlor, the dining room, several bedrooms, the kitchen, and the smokehouse. The former governor's bedroom contains a color lithograph of Thomas Jefferson, as well as personal items belonging to Hogg that were associated with his tenure in office. Located at 1702 North 13th St. in West Columbia.

🅖 ♿ 🏛 🏕 🏠 👣

 **6 BRAZOS BEND STATE PARK**

A section of the floodplain of the Brazos River, this 4,897-acre preserve contains forests, oxbow lakes, coastal prairie, and wetland areas that attract some 270 species of birds, including painted bunting, snowy egret, roseate spoonbill, anhinga, American bittern, great blue heron, white ibis, and the black-bellied whistling duck. The park is also home to American alligators, bobcats, white-tailed deer, raccoons, and gray foxes. There are nine miles of surfaced hiking and bicycle trails, and another 12 miles of unsurfaced trails. Visitors can stroll among groves of live oak, pecan, sycamore, cottonwood, and black willow trees. Archeological evidence shows that the park area has been inhabited by humans as far back as 300 B.C. Located 20 miles southeast of Rosenberg off Hwy. 1462.

🅰 🚻 ♿ 🛏 🏕 👮 🛈 🐻 🚳

 MUSEUM OF FINE ARTS

Located near downtown Houston, this paradigm of modern architecture was the first art museum in the state of Texas. Today the Museum of Fine Arts is one of the nation's major public art galleries. The museum contains more than 27,000 works of art, including Renaissance and Baroque collections, Impressionist and Post-Impressionist art, and the Glassell Collection of African Gold. Outside the museum, the Cullen Sculpture Garden contains works by Henri Matisse, Auguste Rodin, Alberto Giacometti, Louise Bourgeois, and David Smith. Associated with the Museum is Bayou Bend, a gracious Victorian mansion housing a remarkable collection of Early American furniture and decorative arts. The museum is located at 1001 Bissonnet (between Main and Montrose Sts.); Bayou Bend is located at 1 Westcott St.

🅖 ♿ 🏛

Space Center Houston offers a behind-the-scenes tour of the Johnson Space Center, including Rocket Park, above, where visitors can see such famous craft as this mighty Saturn V rocket.

Cypress swamp, left, is one of the diverse environments protected in Big Thicket National Preserve. The region's thick, impenetrable forest discouraged any attempt made to clear it by early settlers, who dubbed it "big thicket."

SANTA CATALINA ISLAND

*A unique corner of wild California
is carefully preserved on this
beloved resort island.*

S anta Catalina rises dramatically from the Pacific Ocean in a continuous ridge of mountains that runs like a spine down the island's length. Oak-lined canyons cut back down to the water, and tiny beaches, clinging to the foot of the cliffs, sometimes harbor a sailboat or two. On some summer mornings, the mountains are capped by epaulets of fog swirling into the 25-mile-wide San Pedro Channel, which separates Catalina from mainland California. At times like this, the rest of the world seems an ocean away.

Most visitors arrive on the regularly scheduled one-hour ferry ride from Long Beach or San Pedro, disembarking at Avalon or Two Harbors. Avalon, the island's only city, is named after a mythical island valley called Avilion in the poem "Idylls of the King" by the English poet Alfred Tennyson. It is a place "where falls not hail nor rain or any snow, nor ever wind blows loudly." Here pedestrians—not cars—dominate the

Overleaf: An aerial view provides a dramatic look at the 21-mile-long chunk of serrated mountains and valleys that form the landscape of Santa Catalina Island.

TILE WORK

An intricate Catalina tile mosaic, below, displays the beauty of this art form. Local artists continue the tradition of tile making, which was once a thriving island industry.

streets. Bright bougainvillea carelessly spills over the whitewashed walls of red-tiled dwellings. Swaying palm trees along the seafront promenade contribute to the city's Mediterranean atmosphere.

The tiny hamlet of Two Harbors is located 25 miles by land—13 miles by boat—west of Avalon in the Isthmus, a half-mile-wide bridge of land that connects the rugged western portion of the island to the larger eastern section. The name comes from the fact that there is a harbor on either side of the narrow neck of land, which rises just 30 feet above sea level. Its twin harbors are often dotted with yachts and sailing boats. The Isthmus has always been a popular getaway place for people who want to avoid the hustle and bustle of Avalon. With its single restaurant, store, and hunting lodge, Two Harbors has little to offer in terms of entertainment but is recognized as one of the best areas for diving in Santa Catalina: its offshore reefs, caves, and kelp forests teem with marine life that beckons underwater enthusiasts to investigate this rich aquatic realm.

WRIGLEY'S HERITAGE

The island's quaint charms, its valleys and mountains, and its beautiful beaches bearing fanciful names such as Wild Boar Gully and Cottonwood Canyon are a poignant reminder of the days when Southern California was still unspoiled by urban sprawl. Santa Catalina was saved from overdevelopment by the farsightedness of William Wrigley, Jr., the chewing gum magnate, who paid $3 million in 1919 for a controlling interest in the island. Wrigley planned to develop a luxury resort but to keep the interior of Catalina in its natural state. In 1929 he built the Casino Building, a lavish Art Deco masterpiece. During the 1930's and 1940's the big bands of Jimmy Dorsey and Benny Goodman, among many others, played here. Downstairs Wrigley opened the Avalon Theatre at the time when talking pictures had just revolutionized the movie industry. Tickets cost a mere 25 cents. Today the colossal 140-foot-high white circular building houses the Catalina Island Museum, located on the ground

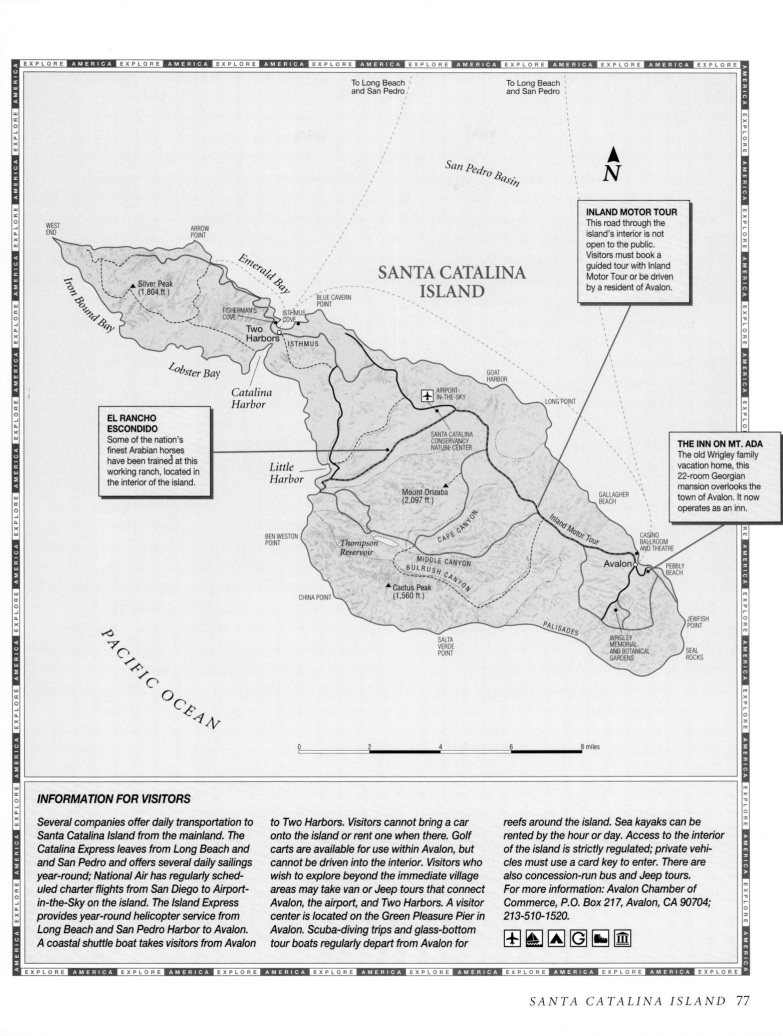

To Long Beach and San Pedro

To Long Beach and San Pedro

San Pedro Basin

N

SANTA CATALINA ISLAND

INLAND MOTOR TOUR
This road through the island's interior is not open to the public. Visitors must book a guided tour with Inland Motor Tour or be driven by a resident of Avalon.

WEST END

ARROW POINT

Emerald Bay

Iron Bound Bay

Silver Peak (1,804 ft.)

FISHERMAN'S COVE

ISTHMUS COVE

BLUE CAVERN POINT

Two Harbors

ISTHMUS

Lobster Bay

Catalina Harbor

GOAT HARBOR

AIRPORT-IN-THE-SKY

LONG POINT

SANTA CATALINA CONSERVANCY NATURE CENTER

EL RANCHO ESCONDIDO
Some of the nation's finest Arabian horses have been trained at this working ranch, located in the interior of the island.

Little Harbor

Mount Orizaba (2,097 ft.)

GALLAGHER BEACH

THE INN ON MT. ADA
The old Wrigley family vacation home, this 22-room Georgian mansion overlooks the town of Avalon. It now operates as an inn.

BEN WESTON POINT

Thompson Reservoir

CAPE CANYON

MIDDLE CANYON

BULRUSH CANYON

Inland Motor Tour

CASINO BALLROOM AND THEATRE

Avalon

PEBBLY BEACH

Cactus Peak (1,560 ft.)

CHINA POINT

PACIFIC OCEAN

SALTA VERDE POINT

PALISADES

WRIGLEY MEMORIAL AND BOTANICAL GARDENS

SEAL ROCKS

JEWFISH POINT

0   2   4   6   8 miles

INFORMATION FOR VISITORS

Several companies offer daily transportation to Santa Catalina Island from the mainland. The Catalina Express leaves from Long Beach and and San Pedro and offers several daily sailings year-round; National Air has regularly scheduled charter flights from San Diego to Airport-in-the-Sky on the island. The Island Express provides year-round helicopter service from Long Beach and San Pedro Harbor to Avalon. A coastal shuttle boat takes visitors from Avalon to Two Harbors. Visitors cannot bring a car onto the island or rent one when there. Golf carts are available for use within Avalon, but cannot be driven into the interior. Visitors who wish to explore beyond the immediate village areas may take van or Jeep tours that connect Avalon, the airport, and Two Harbors. A visitor center is located on the Green Pleasure Pier in Avalon. Scuba-diving trips and glass-bottom tour boats regularly depart from Avalon for reefs around the island. Sea kayaks can be rented by the hour or day. Access to the interior of the island is strictly regulated; private vehicles must use a card key to enter. There are also concession-run bus and Jeep tours. For more information: Avalon Chamber of Commerce, P.O. Box 217, Avalon, CA 90704; 213-510-1520.

floor of the building. The museum houses artifacts of the island's 7,000 years of human history, an art gallery, and memorabilia from the resort's heyday. The rest of the Casino still operates as a ballroom and a theater.

Situated so close to Los Angeles, Santa Catalina soon became a popular resort for movie stars and was a natural magnet for movie scouts sleuthing for natural settings. More than 400 movies have been shot on the island, including *Mutiny on the Bounty* and *Treasure Island*—both of them using the Isthmus as a backdrop.

Although the Wrigleys were aware of Catalina's tourism potential, they were also keenly protective of the island's fragile beauty. In 1972 members of the family created the nonprofit Santa Catalina Island Conservancy, to which three years later they deeded 42,135 acres—all of the interior of the island and 48 miles of coastline. Local inhabitants refer to the Conservancy, which is dedicated to preserving the island's native flora and fauna and unique geographical features, as "in the hills," perhaps because its land is a separate world from the rest of Santa Catalina. The Conservancy operates a Nature Center at the island's dramatic Airport-in-the-Sky, where visitors are greeted by the nostalgic rumble of radial engines on the venerable DC-3's and Beech 18's that regularly haul freight to and from the island. Small private planes also land here. The center provides a brief overview of the island's natural history with displays on its geologic origins, native plants, and animals.

great natural conveyor belt that may eventually carry all of coastal Southern California north to the Gulf of Alaska. Bends along the San Andreas Fault north of Los Angeles are responsible for uneven movement, causing sections of land to be raised in one place, such as Catalina Island, and dropped in others, such as the deep Ventura Basin.

LIVING TREASURES Islands have always acted as nature's experimental stations. Many of Catalina's plants and animals have evolved in a unique way here; others were carried across water or by air from the mainland and from other islands, such as the five Channel Islands, located to the northwest. Nine of Catalina's endemic plants are found nowhere else on earth. Since Europeans first landed on Catalina in 1542, at least another 200 plant species have been introduced, some providing vigorous competition with native vegetation. Near the coast lies the maritime desert scrub with its prickly pear and cholla cacti. The lovely and abundant St. Catherine's lace is aptly named for its white, lacy flowers, which blossom in the summer. The plant, which thrives in the coastal regions, can grow to a height of 10 feet. The charmingly

ADAPTED TO SURVIVE
Succulents like these dudleya, left, are typical of Catalina's maritime desert scrub community.

HOME ON THE RANGE
Catalina is home to many introduced species, the most surprising of which is the bison, seen below. Fourteen of the shaggy animals were brought to the island in 1924 for use in a film. Today their descendants number about 250.

Catalina had a tortuous birth and, in a geological sense, is a different world from the mainland of California. The island was formed more than 100 million years ago when three of the massive plates that form the earth's crust collided, driving seafloor rock and sediment some 25 miles down into the bowels of the earth in a process known as subduction. High temperatures and pressure formed the more than 100-million-year-old metamorphic rocks that comprise the northwestern portion of the island. Volcanic activity, which occurred much later, formed the 1,500-foot-high cliffs of the rugged volcanic peaks that predominate at the island's southeastern end. The result of all of this geological jostling is a 76-square-mile island that is 21 miles long and a little more than 8 miles at its widest, with 54 miles of coastline. Mount Orizaba, the island's highest point, prominently stands 2,097 feet above the surrounding ocean. Winter temperatures typically vary from 50°F to 60°F. Summer temperatures within the island's interior can easily be 10 degrees higher than on the coast. Rainfall averages 14 inches a year, most of it arriving as winter storms.

The product of subduction and volcanism, Santa Catalina Island has been riding on the back of a

named Catalina live forever is a native stonecrop that clings to the dry rocky slopes of the protected coast of the island's northern side. Coast sage scrub, California sagebrush, Catalina bedstraw, and Catalina bush mallow grow at higher elevations. Higher still are the grasslands with their seasonal displays of wildflowers.

The chaparral—a thicket of scrubs and dwarf trees—flourishes on the ridges of the island's north side. Dyer's greenwold—an introduced species of the pea family—has displaced much of the bush lupine and silver lotus that once covered the hillsides. But other endemic island species have been able to maintain a foothold within the chaparral, including the fire-dependent Catalina manzanita: its seeds require heat in order to germinate. The manzanita is just one of many species of plants in the chaparral that returns to life after a fire.

Woodland cloaks the cooler and more moist north-facing slopes of the island. Oak groves are found on the hillsides; cottonwood and willow bosques grow along the streams. The extremely rare Catalina mahogany and the Catalina ironwood trees are living testimony to the successful preservation of the island's indigenous flora. Small groves of the tall, slender Catalina ironwood are found only in the cool, moist environments of the valleys and north-facing slopes of the mountains. The trees, which once flourished on the mainland millions of years ago, are protected from grazing animals within the Conservancy. This subspecies of ironwood grows nowhere else on earth; its only relatives are found on the nearby Channel Islands.

ISLAND RESIDENTS

Mammals and reptiles have also found a home here, but visitors are more likely to see birds and insects. The flightless shield-backed katydid and Avalon hairstreak butterfly live nowhere else on the planet. The Catalina quail is a common sight along the island's roads, running until forced to fly. Despite the ease with which birds should be able to migrate from the mainland, Santa Catalina does not have a diverse bird population. Bald eagles, once decimated by DDT, have been reintroduced to the island and are making a comeback.

Santa Catalina even boasts a population of Southern Pacific rattlesnakes. Their prey includes the Catalina ground squirrel, active during late spring and summer daylight hours, and easily seen by visitors. The island's largest predator is the cat-sized Catalina fox, but its preference for nighttime movement makes the animal more difficult to spot. A large mammal that is hard to miss is the bison, imported to the island during the 1920's for the filming of a Zane Grey novel. After the shooting ended, 14 bison stayed behind, finding the island to their liking. Their descendants can be seen grazing on the hillsides above Little Harbor.

Sea lions and an occasional elephant seal are often spotted basking on shoreline rocks. The University of Southern California operates the Wrigley Marine Science Center at Fisherman's Cove, located adjacent to Two Harbors. The center studies brine shrimp, sea bass, and a host of other marine crea-

MONUMENTAL MEMORIAL
Dedicated to the memory of William Wrigley Jr., the Wrigley Memorial, below, is built almost entirely of native island stone.

tures. Glass-bottom boat tours departing from Avalon treat visitors to sights such as the bright orange garibaldi. Skates and rays sometimes glide past boats as they float over the offshore kelp beds. The Tuna Club, founded in 1898, is the nation's oldest fishing club and is considered to be the birthplace of big-game sportfishing. The island has long been popular as a fishing destination, favored in the past by Charlie Chaplin, John Wayne, and Cecil B. DeMille. Winston Churchill is another famous person who once fished these waters.

People have lived on Santa Catalina for an extremely long time. Some evidence of habitation around Little Harbor dates back 7,000 years. By A.D. 1000 the Pimugnan people were well established here, two of their population centers being the present sites of Avalon and Two Harbors. Using bone harpoons, they harvested the sea's abundance and supplemented their diet with herbs and seeds. The Pimugnans quarried a soapstone called steatite,

FOX COUNTRY
The Santa Catalina Island Conservancy is the habitat of the Catalina fox, left, which grows to the size of a house cat. This inquisitive creature is most often sighted in the late evening.

RELIC OF THE PAST
Old Eagle's Nest, below, was built in the 1880's. It was once a stagecoach stop along the old Farnsworth stage road in Middle Canyon.

Eucalyptus trees provide a perfect frame for one of Santa Catalina's many natural harbors, below. Eucalyptus is not native to the island, but rather is an introduced species that thrives here. Of the 396 species of native flora found on Catalina, nine grow nowhere else on earth.

which they shaped into cookware and effigies; they also traded goods with neighboring peoples.

The first Europeans to visit Santa Catalina arrived in 1542, when Juan Rodriguez Cabrillo, a Spanish navigator in search of a northerly passage connecting the Pacific and Atlantic oceans, dropped anchor and received a warm welcome from the Pimugnans. Cabrillo moved on, and the island was forgotten until it was rediscovered 60 years later by Sebastian Vizcaino. He named the island on November 24, 1602—the eve of the feast of St. Catherine of Alexandria. Both explorers claimed the island for Spain, but for the next 150 years it was virtually ignored. Not until 1769, when the Spanish began to build a string of missions along the coast, did interest in Santa Catalina revive.

With the arrival of European settlers in California, the life of the Pimugnans was to change forever. Many native islanders were taken to mainland Spanish missions; those left behind were subject to the scourges of European diseases. By the 1820's no natives remained, and traders and smugglers moved in to fill the void. A number of mining ventures—including a brief gold rush—were undertaken, with little success. Union army troops were stationed on the Isthmus during the Civil War; the Isthmus Yacht Club now occupies what was formerly their barracks.

George Shatto was an early entrepreneur who made the first attempt to draw visitors to the island. Shatto purchased Catalina in 1887, built Avalon's grand Metropole Hotel, and sold tent sites to vis-

OCEANIC ENCOUNTER
A diver examines a sea urchin, left, and in turn is observed by brightly colored garibaldi, which inhabit the offshore kelp beds. Once an endangered species due to overfishing, the garibaldi is now a common sight in the clear waters surrounding Santa Catalina Island.

itors above Avalon Bay. The island was acquired in 1892 by the Banning brothers, transportation entrepreneurs who opened a golf course—the oldest course still in use in the state—as well as a dance parlor and concert amphitheater. The Bannings also constructed a stage road, which encouraged further development. Resorts sprang up at Little Harbor, Emerald Bay, and Eagle's Nest. In 1915 fire ravaged the Metropole Hotel; it was then that the Wrigleys bought the Bannings' troubled Santa Catalina Island Company.

There is a bench at the end of the road on the south side of Catalina Harbor, across from Two Harbors, where there may be no more poignant vantage point from which to savor the essence of Santa Catalina. Boats at anchor rock softly on the low swells that roll into the harbor, their rigging clanking against their masts. The island's southwestern coast stretches past Little Harbor and Ben Weston Point, waves washing white in the eternal struggle of land against the sea.

Sitting here, contemplating the sunset, a visitor can't help but be mesmerized by the pounding Pacific Ocean, which gleams endlessly westward, and be awed by all the treasures that the island holds in store.

HOME TO ROOST
At nightfall brown pelicans return to roosting sites like the one shown at left. During the day, these seabirds patrol the coast in search of anchovies and other small fish.

NEARBY SITES & ATTRACTIONS

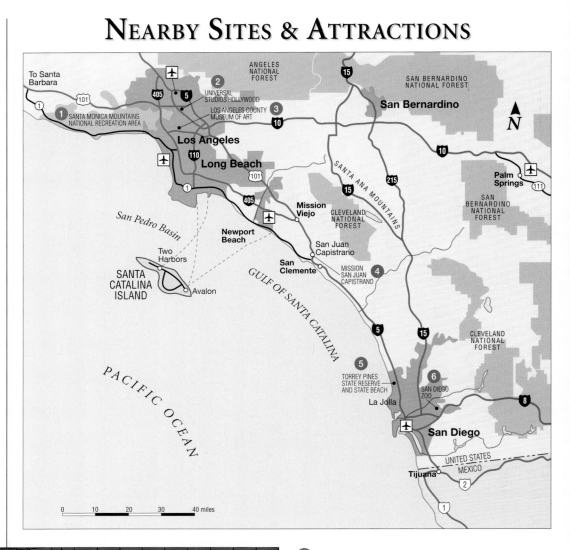

The Serra Chapel at Mission San Juan Capistrano is the only remaining mission church where Father Junípero Serra himself conducted services.

1 SANTA MONICA MOUNTAINS NATIONAL RECREATION AREA

A patchwork of federal, state, county, and municipal parks, Santa Monica Mountains National Recreation Area encompasses one of the nation's few mountain ranges that runs in an east-west direction. This popular recreation area lies on the doorstep of the Los Angeles metropolitan area and features 150,000 acres of mountains, canyons, rolling woodlands, and beaches. On the canyon floors sycamore, willow, and ferns grow in abundance; sections of the canyon walls are lined with chaparral and sage. Elevated sections above the shoreline are studded with valley oak trees. Running for 59 miles through the park, Mulholland Drive provides panoramic views of the surrounding countryside; there are also numerous scenic canyon roads. Fire plays an important role in the natural cycle of the Santa Monica Mountains' chaparral ecosystem: within weeks of such an occurrence, new growth begins in the charred landscape. Three to five years later, the hill-sides are covered with wildflowers, which in turn attract small animals and birds. The area's 46 miles of shoreline alternate between sandy beaches and rocky outcrops. A visitor information center is located off Hwy. 101 in Agoura Hills. Located just west of Los Angeles off Hwys. 1 and 101.

2 UNIVERSAL STUDIOS HOLLYWOOD

The magic of Hollywood movies comes alive during a tour of Universal Studios Hollywood, the biggest and busiest motion picture and television studio in the world. With more than 5 million visitors annually, Universal Studios is one of the most popular tourist attractions in the nation. During the walking portion of the tour, special effects and stunts are displayed. Visitors then board a tram for a ride that takes them through some of the studio's 500 outdoor sets—including "New York Street," "Colonial Street," "Old Mexico Street," and "European Street." The back-lot tram tour also includes "Earthquake—the Big One," "King Kong," and "Jaws." In addition, Universal Studios offers state-of-the-art rides such as "Back to the Future—the Ride" and "The E.T. Adventure," a mysterious trip to the "Green Planet" on the endearing extraterrestrial's flying bicycle. The behind-the-scenes excursion allows visitors to explore special-effects sound stages and view extraordinary stunt shows. Located in Universal City.

3 LOS ANGELES COUNTY MUSEUM OF ART

The largest museum west of the Mississippi, the Los Angeles County Museum of Art boasts more than 150,000 works of art housed in five separate buildings. The most striking of these is the sandstone and glass-brick Anderson Building, which contains the museum's outstanding collection of 20th-century art. In the Ahmanson Building, four gallery levels display works ranging from pre-Columbian art from the Americas to 17th-century Dutch, Flemish, Italian, and Spanish paintings. Sculpture gardens feature 14 bronze sculptures by Auguste Rodin, including the famed *Monument to Balzac*. The Indian and Southeast Asian collection contains more than 5,000 works. The Pavilion for Japanese Art displays hundreds of screen and scroll paintings from the Edo period. Founded in 1910, the museum's collections grew through generous donations and bequests from wealthy patrons, including oil magnate J. Paul Getty and publisher William Randolph Hearst. Located at 5905 Wilshire Blvd. in Los Angeles.

4 MISSION SAN JUAN CAPISTRANO

Known as the jewel of the missions, San Juan Capistrano was founded in 1776 by Father Junípero Serra. The mission, which took its name from the 15th-century Italian theologian St. John of Capistran, was built to convert the Juaneño Indians. The great stone church was destroyed during an 1812 earthquake that killed 40 worshipers, and was never rebuilt. During the 19th century, the mission was seized by the Mexican government and served as a private residence from 1845 to 1865. Today it houses exhibits pertaining to Native American and Spanish colonial life, including a soldiers' barracks, padres' quarters, sacred garden, mission cemetery, and the Serra Chapel—the oldest building in California that is still in use. The mission is best known for the annual return of the swallows on March 19, when birds nest on the walls and arches of the church. Located in San Juan Capistrano.

5 TORREY PINES STATE RESERVE AND STATE BEACH

Although this tree once thrived across the continent, climate change and human encroachment have reduced the habitat of the small Torrey pine—one of the world's rarest species of pine tree—to the southwestern corner of California. Only 6,000 trees survive today—half at this coastal reserve and the other half on Santa Rosa Island, located 175 miles to the north. Only 10 percent of Torrey pine seedlings develop into mature trees. The closed cones open and scatter their nuts only when subjected to heat from fires. The seeds from the pine cones are favored by squirrels and other rodents. The reserve includes eight miles of hiking trails, and picnic areas on the beach, which offers opportunities for swimming, surfing, and whale- and bird-watching. Located 3 miles north of La Jolla on North Torrey Pines Rd.

Pacific Ocean winds have twisted the rare Torrey pine (Pinus torreyana) into shapes that resemble Japanese bonsai.

6 SAN DIEGO ZOO

One of the world's largest and most popular zoos, the San Diego Zoo is noted for its work in breeding rare animals in captivity. Its 100 acres provide a habitat for 900 species of animals, totaling more than 4,000 individual specimens. Animals are separated from each other and from the public by a series of moats, instead of by cages and fences. There is also a walk-through aviary. An aerial tramway provides transportation above the tropical and subtropical landscape as well as a view of Balboa Park, or visitors may take guided tours on double-decker buses. Some of the highlights of the zoo include an impressive population of koalas that cling to eucalyptus trees, Sumatran tigers, Malayan sun bears, reptiles, and primates. The Children's Zoo includes nurseries and petting paddocks specially sized for kids. Located at 2920 Zoo Dr. in San Diego.

Among the many residents of San Diego Zoo's lagoon is this flamingo, which shyly conceals itself behind its rosy pink plumage.

Monterey to Big Sur

---

*Time and the elements together
have molded California's
legendary Pacific playground.*

In 1542 Spanish explorer Juan Cabrillo sailed north along what is now the Big Sur coast and past Monterey Bay. He was disappointed when he saw there were no cities paved with gold—just imposing sea cliffs, forested hills, sandy beaches, and wind-sculpted cypress trees clinging to rugged headlands. Cabrillo and his crew moved on without even landing, never realizing that such a sublime coastline and the fertile waters of the bay itself might constitute a treasure far more valuable than gold.

The Ohlone people had long recognized the value of their home by Monterey Bay, but for 228 years after Cabrillo's passage Europeans remained oblivious to its many splendors. It was not until 1770 that Father Junípero Serra—founder of California's chain of Franciscan missions along the coast—and Gaspar de Portola, the Spanish governor of Alta California, founded the town of Monterey. Although the Monterey Peninsula and the Big Sur coast now are divided into a number of municipalities and are home to some 100,000

TIDE POOL SPECTATORS
Enclosed on three sides and regularly covered by the high tides of the Pacific Ocean, the Great Tide Pool, above, allows visitors at the Monterey Bay Aquarium to view the activities of sea otters and sea lions.

SHORELINE SCULPTURE
Overleaf: Veiled by sea mist and etched by time, the rocks of the Big Sur coast rear up from the Pacific surf like ancient sentinels standing watch on the shore.

people, ample evidence remains from bygone days—as does the sumptuous natural setting.

The Monterey Peninsula includes the city of Monterey and the nearby towns of Pacific Grove and Carmel, as well as the golfing mecca of Pebble Beach. Near the mainland at the south of the peninsula lies the quaint artistic colony of Carmel, site of the mission of San Carlos Borromeo de Carmelo, established by Father Serra in 1770. The state's first and most spectacular scenic drive, Highway 1, runs south from Carmel and down through Big Sur. Dominating the coast are the Santa Lucia Mountains, which rise steeply from the shore to reach heights of more than 3,000 feet.

Travelers can drink deeply of Monterey's early years and its close ties to the sea by following the Path of History—a two-mile walking loop that begins at the Monterey State Historic Park Visitor Center. The park is anchored by the Maritime Museum, an airy new edifice containing seafaring paraphernalia that ranges from a massive first-order lighthouse lens to antique sextants. Across the square lies the Pacific House, one of the weathered adobe buildings characteristic of old Monterey. Several museums occupy this 1847 building. Visitors shouldn't overlook the building's lovely courtyard or the fragrant Sensory Garden behind it. Also on the square is the Monterey Custom House, whose first adobe bricks were laid in the 1820's. The oldest remaining public building in the state, it was the first structure to be placed on California's list of historic landmarks. It was over the Monterey Custom House that Commodore John Drake Sloat raised a flag in 1846 to claim

INFORMATION FOR VISITORS

From the San Francisco Bay Area, take Hwy. 101 to Gilroy and then Hwys. 152 and 1 to Monterey. An alternative route is Hwy. 1 from San Francisco. From Southern California, take Hwy. 101 to Salinas and then Hwy. 68 into Monterey; visitors who wish to see the Big Sur coast may instead take Hwy. 1 north from San Luis Obispo and Morro Bay. There are regularly scheduled flights to and from Monterey Peninsula Airport. From Memorial Day weekend through Labor Day weekend, the city of Monterey operates the WAVE (Waterfront Area Visitors Express), a shuttle bus serving downtown Monterey and major points of interest. The Monterey Bay Aquarium is open year-round. There are 18 private and public golf courses on the peninsula. 17-Mile Drive at Pebble Beach is open from sunrise to sunset; the road runs through private property, so there is an entry fee. The Monterey Visitor Center is located at the corner of Franklin St. and Camino El Estero. The visitor center for Monterey State Historic Park is in Custom House Plaza.

For more information: Monterey Peninsula Visitors & Convention Bureau, P.O. Box 1770, Alvarado St., Monterey, CA 93942-1770; 408-649-1770.

SHIMMERING SQUID
The Monterey Bay Aquarium offers a unique look at the fascinating underwater world and marine life along the bayside coast.

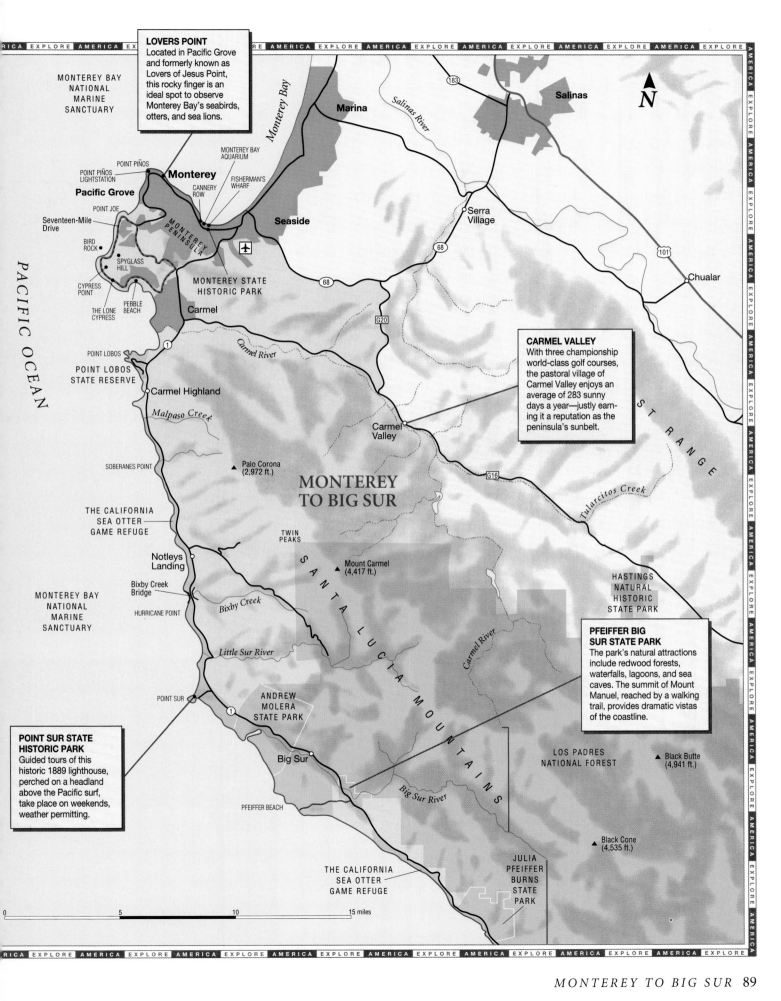

LOVERS POINT
Located in Pacific Grove
and formerly known as
Lovers of Jesus Point,
this rocky finger is an
ideal spot to observe
Monterey Bay's seabirds,
otters, and sea lions.

Monterey Bay

Marina

Salinas River

183

Salinas

N

MONTEREY BAY
AQUARIUM

POINT PIÑOS

POINT PIÑOS
LIGHTSTATION

Monterey

CANNERY
ROW

FISHERMAN'S
WHARF

Pacific Grove

POINT JOE

Seventeen-Mile
Drive

BIRD
ROCK

SPYGLASS
HILL

CYPRESS
POINT

THE LONE
CYPRESS

PEBBLE
BEACH

MONTEREY
PENINSULA

Seaside

Serra
Village

68

68

101

Chualar

MONTEREY STATE
HISTORIC PARK

Carmel

1

POINT LOBOS

POINT LOBOS
STATE RESERVE

Carmel River

G20

CARMEL VALLEY
With three championship
world-class golf courses,
the pastoral village of
Carmel Valley enjoys an
average of 283 sunny
days a year—justly earn-
ing it a reputation as the
peninsula's sunbelt.

PACIFIC OCEAN

Carmel Highland

Malpaso Creek

Carmel
Valley

ST RANGE

SOBERANES POINT

Palo Corona
(2,972 ft.)

**MONTEREY
TO BIG SUR**

G16

Tularcitos Creek

THE CALIFORNIA
SEA OTTER
GAME REFUGE

TWIN
PEAKS

HASTINGS
NATURAL
HISTORIC
STATE PARK

Notleys
Landing

Mount Carmel
(4,417 ft.)

S
A
N
T
A

L
U
C
I
A

M
O
U
N
T
A
I
N
S

Bixby Creek
Bridge

HURRICANE POINT

Bixby Creek

MONTEREY BAY
NATIONAL
MARINE
SANCTUARY

Little Sur River

Carmel River

**PFEIFFER BIG
SUR STATE PARK**
The park's natural attractions
include redwood forests,
waterfalls, lagoons, and sea
caves. The summit of Mount
Manuel, reached by a walking
trail, provides dramatic vistas
of the coastline.

POINT SUR

1

ANDREW
MOLERA
STATE PARK

LOS PADRES
NATIONAL FOREST

Black Butte
(4,941 ft.)

**POINT SUR STATE
HISTORIC PARK**
Guided tours of this
historic 1889 lighthouse,
perched on a headland
above the Pacific surf,
take place on weekends,
weather permitting.

Big Sur

Big Sur River

Black Cone
(4,535 ft.)

PFEIFFER BEACH

JULIA
PFEIFFER
BURNS
STATE
PARK

THE CALIFORNIA
SEA OTTER
GAME REFUGE

0   5   10   15 miles

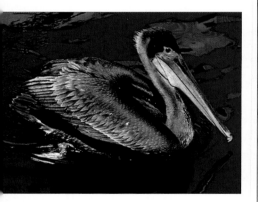

California and much of the West as territory belonging to the United States.

From the waterfront, the Path of History meanders through several blocks to an inland cluster of historic buildings. Foremost is the Royal Presidio Chapel, completed in 1794 and the oldest building in Monterey. The Moorish-style tower and vaulted ceiling of the basilica are impressive, but most remarkable is the spartan cell where Father Serra lived and died: his bed was a slab of wood covered by a single blanket.

Near the end of the Path of History loop lies the old whaling station, an 1847 adobe house complete with a whalebone sidewalk, that marks the time when Monterey's citizens turned their eyes to the sea. Whaling kept Monterey's waterfront hopping from about 1850 to the 1880's.

On the northwestern tip of the peninsula lies the seaside community of Pacific Grove. Founded as a

Methodist retreat in 1875, Pacific Grove has preserved many of its picturesque Victorian homes, which lend a peaceful, turn-of-the-century ambience to the town. Every year millions of orange-and-black monarch butterflies congregate here for the winter, giving rise to Pacific Grove's nickname, "Butterfly Town U.S.A."

More than anything, it was the tiny sardine that shaped Monterey during the early 20th century. The frenetic activity of the sardine fishery was captured most vividly in John Steinbeck's famous 1945 novel, *Cannery Row*. "A poem, a stink, a grating noise, a quality of light, a tone, a habit, a nostalgia" is how Salinas-born Steinbeck characterized life amid the canneries on Ocean View Avenue, renamed Cannery Row in 1958. After World War II, the canneries closed down one by one as the sardines ran out. The husks of several canneries remain in the form of restaurants or shopping complexes, while others sit empty.

The foyer of the Monterey Bay Aquarium preserves three huge boilers and smokestacks of the old Hovden cannery. In the heyday of the canning industry, the stench from the fish was so strong that workers were compelled to burn their clothes every six weeks. A shabby, unmarked building near the aquarium once served as the laboratory of biologist Ed Ricketts, Steinbeck's closest friend and the model for the character of Doc in *Cannery Row*. The Wing Chong Market, which Steinbeck described in the novel as a "miracle of supply," now houses an antique shop with an extensive collection of Steinbeck memorabilia. Cannery Row offers much for visitors in addition to memories of Steinbeck and sardines. During the summer people throng the bazaar of shops, restaurants, and art galleries along the mile-long street.

HISTORIC WHARF
The former hub of the local fishing industry, Fisherman's Wharf, below, now belongs to tour operators offering sightseeing, fishing, and whale-watching tours of Monterey Bay.

The benign climate of Pacific Grove provides a perfect wintering site for the monarch butterfly, right. Millions of these fragile travelers migrate here annually to escape the cold weather.

COASTAL COLONY

Because the waters around Monterey Peninsula are protected as part of Monterey Bay National Marine Sanctuary, sea lion colonies, such as the one below, have flourished here in recent years.

LILIES BY THE SEA

Big Sur's temperate climate, influenced by the warm Japan Current offshore, encourages the growth of a wide variety of shrubs and flowers, such as these delicate calla lilies, opposite page. The steep Santa Lucia Mountains help to retain moisture in the coastal zone.

tures, including crabs, starfish, sea slugs, otters, and leopard sharks.

The opening of the Outer Bay wing in 1996 was a milestone event: the new exhibit area shows life in the sunlight zone of the open ocean, a monumental technical feat that no other aquarium has ever managed. Behind a 15- by 54-foot acrylic panel—the largest window in the world—swim some of the big sea creatures that smaller tanks can't hold, such as blue sharks, schools of tuna, pelagic stingrays, and ocean sunfish, the sunfish growing as large as two tons.

The aquarium acquaints visitors with the natural treasures of the coast and bay—a bounty that serves as the foundation for so much work and play. The entire bay, as well as the coastal waters extending from the Golden Gate all the way down to Cambria, now make up the Monterey Bay National Marine Sanctuary, dedicated in 1992. One of the stars of this preserve—the largest of its kind in the United States—is the California sea otter, which has experienced a tremendous resurgence in population since its near-extinction in the 1930's.

Motorists who take Monterey's renowned 17-Mile Drive may start out eager to see the famed golf courses, extravagant homes, and luxurious resorts, but they end up talking about the sea otters they saw off Point Joe and the dizzying swirl of cormorants, gulls, and pelicans at Bird Rock. Those travelers who wish to see more can get an even closer view of ocean life by going out on the water. On a calm day in Monterey Bay, kayakers can quietly pass within 50 feet of boisterous sea lion colonies and otters wrapped up in strands of kelp. A couple of kayak outfitters conduct natural history tours that provide an up-close examination of the life of the bay. When the tour group stops to watch a sea otter cracking a crab on a rock, the guide may mention that sea otters cling to their personal rocks the way King Midas clung to gold, often keeping the same one for years. Guides may also draw attention to some of the sea's hidden booty, perhaps by hauling up some kelp and pointing out a luminous melibe sea slug or a kelp crab that has turned red as a result of its diet.

Boat trips take visitors farther out into the bay during the warm summer months, as well as from December to May, the months when the gray whales migrate. Marine biologist guides show passengers many animals in addition to sea lions, gray whales, sea otters, and other near-shore dwellers. In late summer and fall, blue whales—the largest animals ever to live on earth—come to feed in the bay's nutrient-rich waters. Dolphins range all over the bay, sometimes traveling in groups of up to several hundred. On almost every trip some dolphins will ride the boat's bow wave. Summer also

LIFE IN THE BAY

The biggest attraction today on Cannery Row is the sprawling Monterey Bay Aquarium. Its innovative displays of the sea life that lives in the bay placed it among the world's leading aquariums from the day it opened in 1985. One of the aquarium's highlights is the Kelp Forest, a three-story re-creation of Monterey Bay's huge kelp beds. The towering kelp plants anchor themselves to the seabed and can reach heights of up to 100 feet. The kelp beds nourish and provide a habitat for a host of marine crea-

SOARING REDWOODS
Coastal redwoods attracted the first settlers, who were mainly loggers, to Big Sur in the late 1800's. Groves of redwoods still survive in several nature preserves along the coast.

brings hundreds of humpback whales to the bay. They are the premier leapers among large whales, and—if they are lucky—travelers might see a whale breach (launch itself out of the water) and come crashing back down, reentering the ocean with a mighty splash.

GOLFER'S PARADISE
The legendary golf courses of Pebble Beach lend credence to the self-proclaimed title of "the golf capital of the world." Three of the peninsula's 18 courses in particular —Pebble Beach, Spyglass Hill, and Cypress Point— are widely considered to be among the top 10 courses in the world.

The golf mania carries over into Carmel, where there's even an art gallery devoted solely to golf. Visitors will find many memorable surprises in this enchanting little village. Notable is the Carmel Art Association Gallery, which features a delightful front-yard sculpture garden that makes a peaceful place to relax after a day's sightseeing.

Just a mile south of Carmel lies Point Lobos State Reserve. Scottish novelist Robert Louis Stevenson, who made his home in Monterey during the 1870's, called Point Lobos "the most beautiful meeting of land and sea on earth." Trails lead visitors along the rims of granite sea cliffs, where husky Pacific breakers roll in and ram against the rocks in their age-old quest to batter stone into sand. In protected coves lucid jade-green water dances and sparkles in the sun. Sea otters cruise amid the kelp, and harbor seals drape their sausagelike torsos over offshore rocks. The South Shore Trail slopes downward to sea level, providing access to the rocky beach and tidepools. Bearing in mind the slippery rocks and crashing waves, visitors can search out hermit crabs, sea anemones, barnacles, sea stars, and other residents of this realm that occupies a place midway between land and sea.

Heading south from Point Lobos, the wilds of Big Sur lie ahead. For the Spanish this was El Sur Grande—The Big South. To experience the essence of this breathtakingly magnificent landscape, innumerable clifftop pullouts strung out the length of Highway 1 provide wide-angle views of the steep mountains that thrust up from the ocean. From these lofty vantage points, fortunate travelers are likely to spot migrating gray whales between December and May.

Although the harshness of the coast discouraged Spanish settlers, around the turn of the century a handful of hardy pioneers came to Big Sur to cut redwoods. Groves of these mighty trees—the tallest in the world—still remain, most notably in Pfeiffer Big Sur State Park. Overland travel along the Big Sur coast was all but impossible until 1937, when

the final miles of Highway 1 were carved out of the steep cliffs of the Santa Lucia Mountains. This daredevil strip of blacktop, flamboyantly curving high above the pounding Pacific surf, was declared California's first Scenic Highway and remains the coast's biggest draw.

Big Sur's renowned artistic community was established early in the 20th century, when poets, painters, and other artists from San Francisco fled the destruction of the 1906 earthquake. Writers and artists alike were inspired by the landscape's solitude and beauty. The bohemian community peaked during the 1940's and 1950's, when such people as novelist Henry Miller and nature photographers Edward Weston and Ansel Adams made their homes here. In recent years this coastal region has developed into one of the America's most celebrated playgrounds.

From the less precipitous stretches of Highway 1, side roads and trails provide opportunities to get closer to the water. Several trails in Andrew Molera State Park snake through the cottonwoods and ferns of the interior to two miles of pristine beach. Those who choose to venture out amid the seashells and driftwood must be careful not to get trapped against the base of the bluffs by the incoming tide. A safer bet is the trail that runs along the top of the bluffs, where one can see the harbor seals and watch the oystercatchers hunting for dinner. Farther south, Pfeiffer Beach presents a colossal offshore sculpture garden strewn with rock pillars, arches, and scoured tunnels.

The wonders of Big Sur cast a spell on all who pass this way. This rugged coast richly deserves Henry Miller's famous description: "This is the face of the earth as the Creator intended it to look."

LONG-STANDING BEACON
Point Piños Lightstation began operation in 1855, warning ships off the reefs of the Monterey Peninsula. Now also a museum, this is the oldest continuously operating lighthouse on the West Coast.

SECLUDED HAVEN
A sheltered cove reveals an undersea kelp bed, part of the tangled jungle that nourishes the rich and complex marine life of Monterey Bay and the Big Sur coast.

Nearby Sites & Attractions

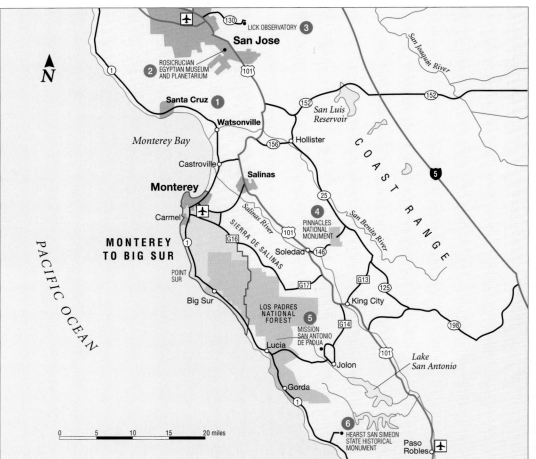

The rock spires of Pinnacles National Monument are remnants of an ancient volcano. Some geologists claim that erosion has reduced the mountain to about a third of its original height.

Swimmers enjoy the surf at Natural Bridges State Beach. The park is named for sandstone bridges that were created by the force of the tides.

1 SANTA CRUZ

Originally established as a Franciscan mission in 1791, Santa Cruz today is a popular seaside resort with a large artisan population. The city's boardwalk amusement park—one of the few of its kind left in the world—includes a casino built in 1907, a 1911 carousel, and a vintage 1920's roller coaster. The highlight of Santa Cruz's 29 miles of public beaches is Natural Bridges State Beach, where the pounding of the waves has carved three connected rock bridges out of a sandstone cliff. The park's monarch butterfly preserve is home to millions of monarchs every winter. Located on Hwy. 1.

2 ROSICRUCIAN EGYPTIAN MUSEUM AND PLANETARIUM

This substantial collection of Egyptian artifacts—both original and reconstructed—is one of the largest of its kind in the western United States. Modeled after the Temple of Amon at Karnak, Egypt, it is the only Egyptian museum in the world housed in Egyptian-style architecture. The museum has nine mummies, which include priests, a fish, and a cat. There are also displays of pottery, jewelry, tools, alabaster vessels, and Coptic textiles. Outside stands the statue of Tuart, the half-hippopotamus, half-crocodile god who was the protector of women in pregnancy and childbirth. Adjacent to the museum is one of the oldest planetariums in the nation, built in 1936. Its theater has shows that feature all the planets in the earth's solar system, as well as more than 2,000 stars. Located at 1342 Naglee Ave. in San Jose.

③ LICK OBSERVATORY

Perched on the lofty summit of 4,209-foot Mount Hamilton, the University of California's Lick Observatory contains seven telescopes, including some of the world's most powerful. The observatory is named after James Lick, a wealthy San Franciscan who established the first permanently occupied mountain observatory in the world in 1876. Lick wanted to build a telescope more powerful than any that had previously been constructed. The 36-inch refractor installed by Lick in 1888 remains the second-largest refractor in the world today. The observatory's most powerful telescope is the Shane 120-inch reflector; its impressive mirror measures 10 feet in diameter and is polished to an accuracy of better than 1/1,000,000 of an inch. Photographs are on display in the visitors gallery. Located 19 miles east of San Jose on Hwy. 130.

④ PINNACLES NATIONAL MONUMENT

East of the smooth rolling hills of the Salinas Valley rear the sharp spires, caves, and rocky outcrops of the aptly named Pinnacles National Monument. Established in 1908, the monument is composed of the remnants of a 23-million-year-old volcano adjacent to the San Andreas Fault. The movement of the fault, combined with heat, wind, frost, and water erosion, produced these rugged rock formations. The pinnacles are complemented by colorful plant life. Deeper soils support groves of sycamore, oak, and buckeye, and the rockier areas host plant life known as chaparral, whose seeds germinate only after they have been opened by the extreme heat of fire. These plants include chamise, buckbrush, and manzanita. Among the animals that inhabit the region are elusive bobcats, coyotes, and gray foxes, along with more frequently sighted black-tailed deer, rabbits, beechy ground squirrels, and raccoons. Birds include California quails, scrub jays, turkey vultures, and acorn woodpeckers. The monument can be seen by means of numerous hiking trails. Park headquarters and the Bear Gulch Visitor Center are located 32 miles south of Hollister on Hwy. 146 off Hwy. 25; the Chaparral Visitor Center is located 14 miles east of Soledad on Hwy. 146.

⑤ MISSION SAN ANTONIO DE PADUA

Nestled in the foothills of the Santa Lucia Mountains, Mission San Antonio de Padua was third in the chain of 21 missions established by the Spanish to convert California's Native Americans to Christianity. The mission was founded in 1771, but construction of the present main church did not begin until 1810. The mission was notable as the site of California's first aqueduct, first water-powered gristmill, first tile roof, and first Christian marriage ceremony. Partially restored in the early 1900's, the mission was returned to its original appearance in 1948 following major

restoration work sponsored by the Franciscan Order. Today the mission is a parish of the Catholic Church, maintained by the Franciscans. The church and museum are open to visitors, who may also tour the barracks, reservoir, and gristmill ruins. Located at Fort Hunter Liggett about 5 miles north of Jolon.

⑥ HEARST SAN SIMEON STATE HISTORICAL MONUMENT

In 1921 newspaper tycoon William Randolph Hearst asked architect Julia Morgan to help make his San Simeon property "more comfortable." Accordingly, she designed a European-style castle that Hearst named the Enchanted Hill. Set atop a 1,600-foot hill overlooking the Pacific Ocean, the castle is an imposing sight. Due to its size, four separate tours are needed to view it in entirety. The main building, called Casa Grande, includes a billiard room, a library, a movie theater, tennis courts, two Roman-style swimming pools, and a dining-room table that can seat 22. Materials and artwork used in the castle's construction include French Gothic doors, Persian tiles, Byzantine courtyard fonts, Veronese marble, and Italian Renaissance choir stalls. A walk through any room, garden, or terrace passes by extravagant paintings, vases, and statues, such as a 3,400-year-old bust of the Egyptian goddess Sekhmet. Located 14 miles south of Gorda off Hwy 1.

One of California's unique landmarks, Hearst San Simeon State Historical Monument towers above the surrounding hills. Hearst's dream home was donated to the state in 1958.

The Olympic Peninsula

Pristine shoreline, wilderness, and historic port towns beguile visitors to the Olympic Peninsula.

Whitecapped breakers ram against the shoreline rocks and explode into glittering fragments while dapper sandpipers mince along the water's edge, taking care to stay just out of reach of the ocean's frothy fingers. The sand hisses softly as the waves wash back to the ocean. Like surgeons wielding scalpels, oystercatchers use their long orange bills to slice open mussels. Immediately above the high-tide line hovers the forest—a verdant riot of strapping conifers webbed with ferns, mosses, and vines.

The Olympic Peninsula is the northwestern-most point of the continental United States. This 50-by-75-mile chunk of Washington State is bounded by the Pacific Ocean on the west, the Strait of Juan de Fuca on the north, and Puget Sound on the east. Much of the peninsula's shoreline is only sparsely settled; the rest is virtually unpopulated, including a long strip that is part of Olympic National Park. Deserted beaches far outnumber towns, and the outposts of civilization

ANCIENT ETCHINGS
Makah Indian petroglyphs, such as the whale and human faces above, are carved on rocks along the western coast of the Olympic Peninsula. Originally whale hunters, the Makah settled the peninsula at least a thousand years before Europeans discovered the region.

SAFE HARBOR
Overleaf: In early morning, the still waters of La Push Harbor reflect the tranquillity of this fishing village. La Push has a long history: Quileute Indians have occupied the area for more than 800 years.

that do exist derive much of their character from the coast. While driving along the shore, visitors may see fishing boats unloading their catch; the reservations of several Native American tribes whose cultures are steeped in sea and shore; and marinas crowded with the boats of weekend anglers. Even in Port Angeles—by far the Olympic Peninsula's largest community, with about 18,000 residents—activity revolves around the town's busy deep-water harbor.

Visitors heading north on Highway 101 up the Pacific Coast get their first taste of the Olympic shore around Kalaloch, a small town with a general store, gas station, ranger station, and a classic rustic lodge perched on a bluff above the water. Kalaloch lies near the southern end of Olympic National Park's coastal stretch, whose 57 wild miles constitute the longest undeveloped shoreline in the lower 48 states. Huge driftwood logs lie by the thousands on the sandy beach as if tossed there by a giant playing pick-up-sticks. Indeed, the stormy Pacific—a grievously misnamed ocean—wields more power than any mythical giant ever could.

The 10-mile stretch of Highway 101 anchored by Kalaloch is the only place on the peninsula's ocean coast where a road runs along the shore for any significant distance. Even there, motorists curving along the bluffs only occasionally get to feast on panoramas of the Pacific; usually a thin but dense veil of forest blocks the view. Roadside pullouts provide one solution, but it's better to take advantage of some of the easy walking trails that lead through the forest strip to grand overlooks or

INFORMATION FOR VISITORS

The main route around the Olympic Peninsula is Hwy. 101; both Aberdeen and Olympia are convenient starting points for a tour of the peninsula. There are several entrances to Olympic National Park, but the main entrance and visitor center are located in Port Angeles. From the park's Ozette Visitor Center, hiking trails lead to the Pacific Ocean at Cape Alava and Sand Point. The Makah Indian Reservation is located at Neah Bay; the Makah Research and Cultural Center is open year-round (daily in summer; Wednesday to Sunday the rest of the year). From Seattle, ferry services via Winslow and Kingston serve the eastern side of the peninsula. There are also daily ferry services between Port Angeles and Victoria, British Columbia, and between Port Townsend and Whidbey Island. There are major airports in Seattle-Tacoma, Olympia, Aberdeen, and Port Angeles.
For more information: North Olympic Peninsula Visitor & Convention Bureau, P.O. Box 670, Port Angeles, WA 98362; 360-452-8552 or 800-942-4042.

TIDEPOOL INHABITANTS
Giant green anemones look like purple-tipped flowers when they spread out their sticky tentacles to feed. These polyp-type creatures thrive in tidepools and along rocky shorelines.

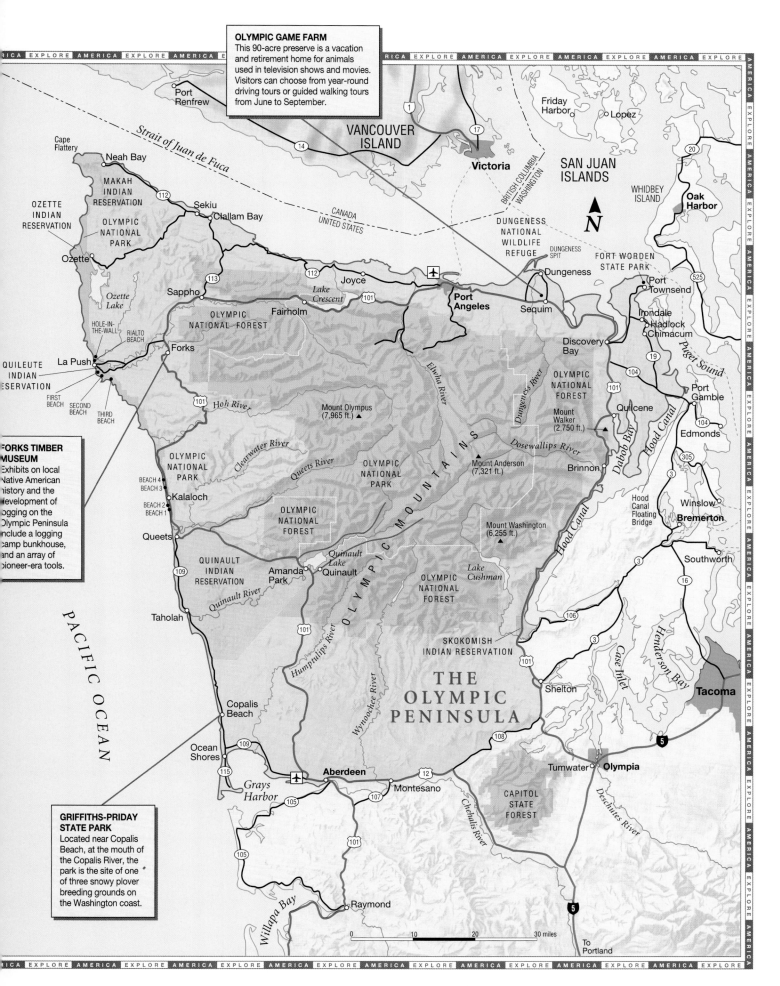

OLYMPIC GAME FARM
This 90-acre preserve is a vacation and retirement home for animals used in television shows and movies. Visitors can choose from year-round driving tours or guided walking tours from June to September.

VANCOUVER ISLAND

Port Renfrew

Strait of Juan de Fuca

Cape Flattery

Neah Bay

MAKAH INDIAN RESERVATION

OZETTE INDIAN RESERVATION

OLYMPIC NATIONAL PARK

Sekiu

Clallam Bay

Ozette

Ozette Lake

HOLE-IN-THE-WALL

RIALTO BEACH

Sappho

113

112

Lake Crescent

Joyce

Fairholm

OLYMPIC NATIONAL FOREST

Forks

FORKS TIMBER MUSEUM
Exhibits on local Native American history and the development of logging on the Olympic Peninsula include a logging camp bunkhouse, and an array of pioneer-era tools.

QUILEUTE INDIAN RESERVATION

La Push

FIRST BEACH

SECOND BEACH

THIRD BEACH

Hoh River

101

Mount Olympus (7,965 ft.) ▲

Clearwater River

Queets River

OLYMPIC NATIONAL PARK

BEACH 4

BEACH 3

Kalaloch

BEACH 2

BEACH 1

OLYMPIC NATIONAL FOREST

Queets

OLYMPIC NATIONAL FOREST

QUINAULT INDIAN RESERVATION

Amanda Park

Quinault Lake

Quinault

Quinault River

Taholah

109

OLYMPIC MOUNTAINS

OLYMPIC NATIONAL PARK

Mount Anderson (7,321 ft.) ▲

Mount Washington (6,255 ft.) ▲

Lake Cushman

OLYMPIC NATIONAL FOREST

SKOKOMISH INDIAN RESERVATION

101

THE OLYMPIC PENINSULA

PACIFIC OCEAN

Copalis Beach

Ocean Shores

115

109

Grays Harbor

105

GRIFFITHS-PRIDAY STATE PARK
Located near Copalis Beach, at the mouth of the Copalis River, the park is the site of one of three snowy plover breeding grounds on the Washington coast.

Humptulips River

Wynoochee River

Aberdeen

107

Montesano

12

108

Chehalis River

CAPITOL STATE FOREST

Tumwater ● **Olympia**

Deschutes River

105

101

Willapa Bay

Raymond

To Portland

VANCOUVER ISLAND

Victoria

BRITISH COLUMBIA / WASHINGTON

CANADA / UNITED STATES

Friday Harbor

Lopez

SAN JUAN ISLANDS

WHIDBEY ISLAND

Oak Harbor

1

17

14

20

N

DUNGENESS NATIONAL WILDLIFE REFUGE

DUNGENESS SPIT

Dungeness

Port Angeles

Sequim

FORT WORDEN STATE PARK

Port Townsend

525

Irondale

Hadlock

Chimacum

19

Discovery Bay

OLYMPIC NATIONAL FOREST

104

101

Port Gamble

Quilcene

Mount Walker (2,750 ft.) ▲

Dosewallips River

Dungeness River

Elwha River

Brinnon

Dabob Bay

Hood Canal

Hood Canal Floating Bridge

Puget Sound

Edmonds

305

3

Winslow

Bremerton

Southworth

16

106

3

Shelton

Case Inlet

Henderson Bay

Tacoma

5

5

0　　10　　20　　30 miles

OLYMPIC HEIGHTS

Towering Douglas fir, western hemlock, Sitka spruce, and western red cedar trees, right, thrive in the old-growth rain forest that continues to grow along the unspoiled coastal strip of Olympic National Park. Closer to the ground, a river otter, below, peeks out from verdant vegetation. This versatile mammal spends part of its time in the water and part on land.

down to the beach. Gray whales and sea otters ply these waters, and sea lions and bird colonies alike occupy some of the rocks. Rich with life and unspoiled by human activity, the western portion of the peninsula's nearshore environment is protected by the Olympic Coast National Marine Sanctuary, established July 16, 1994.

REALM OF TIDEPOOLS

On the beaches, visitors should not neglect to explore the tidepools that are exposed at low tide. It's important to exercise caution, however: slippery algae coats many of the rocks; "sneaker" waves can catch tidepoolers who forget to keep an eye on the sea; and a rising tide can cut off the unwary from the beach. Anyone unfamiliar with tidepooling should consult with park personnel or go on one of the tidepool walks led by ranger-naturalists.

The rocks at the north end of Beach 4 make an excellent tidepool: here millions of tiny animals are eating, fighting, mating, giving birth, and dying. A lucky visitor may come across a sunflower sea star. Two feet across and a radiant mosaic of yellow, orange, red, and purple, they are capable of crawling nearly six feet in a minute—20 times faster than their ocher cousins. Lugging their latest scrounged shells, hermit crabs scamper around the bottoms of the tidepools, careful to avoid the stinging tentacles of the anemones. Discerning tidepoolers who take the time to look past the profusion of relatively large creatures such as barnacles, turban snails, and limpets may spy nudibranchs. A kind of marine mollusk, these creatures have been called the "butterflies of the sea." Typically less than an inch long, they make up for their diminutive stature with bizarre beauty.

The only other portion of the coastal section of the park that can be reached by car is the area around La Push–Rialto Beach. Slipping through the Olympic National Forest, the road splits about five miles from the coast. The south fork passes short trails to Third Beach, Second Beach, and First Beach before ending in the village of La Push, on the Quileute Indian Reservation.

The north fork of the road leads down to Rialto Beach, but along the way visitors should pull over on the bank of the Quillayute River estuary. A survey of the eelgrass beds, sandbars, and the river channel is likely to reveal ducks, great blue herons, and often bald eagles. Depending on the season, as many as a dozen eagles may be diving for fish, soaring above the water, or flirting with each other in aerial courtship, occasionally locking talons and spiraling downwards.

By hiking one-and-a-half miles north along Rialto Beach to Hole-in-the-Wall, visitors can sample the 57-mile wilderness corridor that only a few hardy backpackers see in its entirety. It's at once serene and boisterous: to the west rocks stand toe-to-toe with the surf, absorbing an unending flurry of resounding body blows; to the east arises a green wall of forest, profoundly silent but for the occasional call of a bird, the moss-muffled footfall of a deer, or the murmur of the wind. As travelers trek through the soft, dark sand, they can admire the sensuous grain of driftwood logs or the fanciful curves of stranded sea shells. At Hole-in-the-Wall, low tides reveal an expansive sheet of stone riddled with life-filled pools and fissures. Sometimes raccoons, river otters, and bald eagles surprise beachcombers by showing up here. The proximity of the forest even brings black bears down to the beach.

The officially designated wilderness area is confined to the peninsula's Pacific Ocean side, but nearly wild stretches can be found along its other shores. Curling out into the Strait of Juan de Fuca, for example, is the Dungeness Spit—the world's longest natural spit and the centerpiece of the

VICTORIAN SEAPORT
Port Townsend's outstanding collection of Victorian homes and commercial buildings were built during the late 1800's. British explorer Capt. George Vancouver discovered the natural harbor here in 1792 and named it after his friend, the marquis of Townshend.

Rock formations called sea stacks stand sentinel along a stretch of the coast. Erosion has separated these miniature mountains from the Pacific shoreline.

DOWN-EAST FLAVOR

The architecture of Port Gamble resembles that of a traditional New England town. Port Gamble was founded by Capt. William Talbot of East Machias, Maine, who built a sawmill here in 1853 and modeled many of the town's buildings after those in his hometown.

Dungeness National Wildlife Refuge. This finger of sand, laced with driftwood, hooks six miles into the quiet waters of the strait. The shallows and mudflats on the inside curve attract harbor seals, loons, egrets, and—in the spring and fall—great squabbling flocks of waterfowl and shorebirds.

Traveling along the long stretch of Highway 112 that hugs the coast between Neah Bay and the salmon-fishing town of Sekiu, travelers often spot bald eagles amid the tidepools; dozens of these birds roost here from February through April. A rare albino eagle also lives in the area. Sekiu's sister town, Clallam Bay, offers tidepooling with a twist at its county park: the reef that is near the town's lighthouse has yielded some of the oldest marine fossils in existence, some of which have been named after the local people who found them.

The sea stars and seals and gulls have been sharing the shore of the strait with human inhabitants for a long time. For thousands of years a number of Native American tribes lived off this rich confluence of sea and forest; half a dozen still do. The most accessible of their reservations belong to the

Makah Nation. Some 1,400 Makah occupy the northwestern tip of the Olympic Peninsula, which looks out on both the open Pacific Ocean and the Strait of Juan de Fuca.

BURIED VILLAGE

The highlight of a visit to the Makah Reservation derives from a natural catastrophe: about 500 years ago, a mudslide buried a nearby Makah village, preserving the longhouses and thousands of artifacts. In 1970 tidal erosion uncovered this treasure trove, which is now on display in the excellent Makah Museum. Visitors can see shimmering abalone jewelry, the 30-foot cedar dugout canoes in which crews of eight Makah men went to sea in search of whales, skirts made of thin strips of cedar, and elaborately carved totem poles. Among the fascinating nuggets of information accompanying each exhibit, visitors learn, for example, that after harpooning a whale, Makah hunters would dive overboard and sew up the whale's mouth so the enormous creature would remain afloat while it was towed back to the vil-

lage. The meat and skin of whales (and later seals) formed the basis for Makah traditional culture.

The way of life of the ancient Makah comes to life most vividly in the full-scale reproduction of a cedar longhouse, their traditional dwelling. Dark, cool, and spacious, the longhouse contains an array of typical household items, such as dried salmon strips hanging from the beams and half-woven baskets waiting to be completed.

The twin towns of Sekiu and Clallam Bay, settled by loggers, fishermen, and homesteaders during the 19th century, today draw sport fishermen from far and wide. The tiny community of Joyce is known for the wild blackberry pies served in its two restaurants and for its historic general store, whose wooden floor has been deeply worn by a century's worth of tromping boots. Heading east out of Joyce on Highway 112, motorists may smile at the sight of a sign that reminds them to "Come Back and Re-Joyce."

The only community on the Olympic Peninsula that may rate the title of "city" is Port Angeles. A generally unremarkable place from a tourist's point of view, Port Angeles does have a waterfront that warrants a visit. The observation tower on the end of the city pier affords eagle's-nest views of its magnificent natural harbor, which serves seagoing vessels from around the world.

Jutting from the northeast corner of the Olympic Peninsula is the Quimper Peninsula, at the northern tip of which sits Port Townsend, a comely town of more than 7,900 souls that looks out both on the strait and Puget Sound. Port Townsend's strate-

PEACEFUL SANCTUARY
An elk grazes by early morning light in the Northwest Trek Wildlife Park, outside Tacoma. With an area of more than 600 acres, the park shelters fauna indigenous to the Pacific Northwest.

gic position led to the founding of Fort Worden at about the turn of the century, on the site of an earlier stronghold built in 1855 during hostilities with local Indians. One of three forts in the "Iron Triangle" established to control the approaches to Puget Sound—the others being forts Casey and Flagler—Fort Worden was named in honor of Adm. John L. Worden, who commanded the Union ironclad *Monitor* during its famous battle with the *Merrimac* on March 9, 1862. The fort is now a state park, and visitors can tour the military museum, barracks, and the old artillery emplacements. Also within the park is the Port Townsend Marine Science Center, where visitors can get acquainted with the wealth of sea creatures that inhabit the north coast of the Olympic Peninsula.

Port Townsend's main attraction is its historic district, which dates back to the town's heyday in the 1880's, when it was called the "Key City of Puget Sound" and rivaled Tacoma and Seattle as one of the busiest ports in the Pacific Northwest. Not only do Port Townsend's waterfront and the heights above it enjoy an intriguing past, but also many of the venerable buildings and some Victorian seaport ambience remain. Much of the old town is designated a national historic landmark, including more than 70 buildings—most of them still in use as galleries, restaurants, hotels, and shops.

Dozens of Port Townsend's fine old homes display elegant and extravagant features, such as the 1889-vintage Ann Starrett Mansion, whose three-tiered spiral staircase is topped off with an eight-

TIDAL SCULPTURE
The force of the sea has sculpted the rocks at Rialto Beach into fluted masterpieces. Twice a day low tide uncovers this sculpture garden.

paneled dome covered with frescoes, which function as a solar calendar. Guided walking tours of the historic district reveal some of Port Townsend's shady past, such as the secret "shanghai" doors at the backs of many buildings, where unsuspecting men were dragged out to serve as sailors for unscrupulous ships' captains. Guides point out the many old waterfront businesses whose upper floors used to house brothels, inspiring in part the local maxim: "Sin flourishes at sea level."

When in Port Townsend, one is never too removed from the natural world. Birds abound at the town's 100-acre Kah Tai Lagoon Nature Park, and visitors who take guided kayak trips from the marina may see killer whales spouting in the Strait of Juan de Fuca.

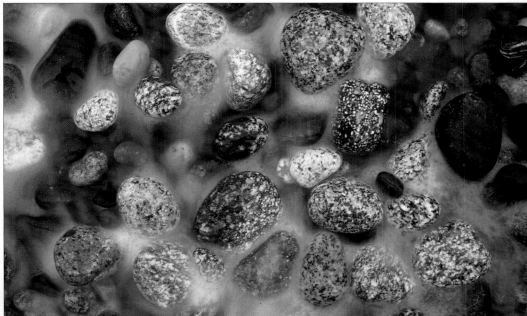

THE EASTERN SHORE

By contrast with the Pacific shore, the eastern side of the Olympic Peninsula presents a more settled appearance. From Port Townsend, visitors can either head back to Bremerton, Tacoma, and Seattle over the Hood Canal Floating Bridge or meander along a scenic stretch of Highway 101, which hugs the western bank of the canal (not a man-made waterway but a long tidal channel). The one-and-a-half-mile-long Hood Canal Floating Bridge—opened in 1961 and rebuilt after a 1979 storm sank part of it—is the world's third-longest floating bridge and the longest built over tidal waters.

South of Port Townsend, an interesting side trip runs along Highway 16 through the historic towns of Hadlock, Chimacum, and Irondale—all well worth a visit. Hadlock was once a prosperous lumber port, and many of its old buildings are still standing in Old Hadlock. Chimacum takes its name from the Indian tribe that formerly lived in the area, and in 1889 Irondale boasted Washington's only iron smelter.

Farther down the 80-mile Hood Canal, the town of Quilcene on Dabob Bay is renowned for its tiny Olympia oysters, which thrive in the cold waters of the bay. Twelve miles south of Quilcene lies the village of Brinnon, home to Whitney Gardens, which showcases a diverse sample of Washington State's official flower, the rhododendron.

South of Quilcene, Mount Walker Viewpoint offers travelers panoramic views of 2,750-foot Mount Walker, as well as sweeping vistas of Mount Rainier, the Cascade Mountains, and the majestic Olympic Mountains, in a fitting final glimpse of this union of sea and mountains.

PLENITUDE OF PEBBLES
Their multihued surfaces a textbook of geology, these beach pebbles in Skagit Bay have been tumbled smooth by the waves that batter the Olympic coastline.

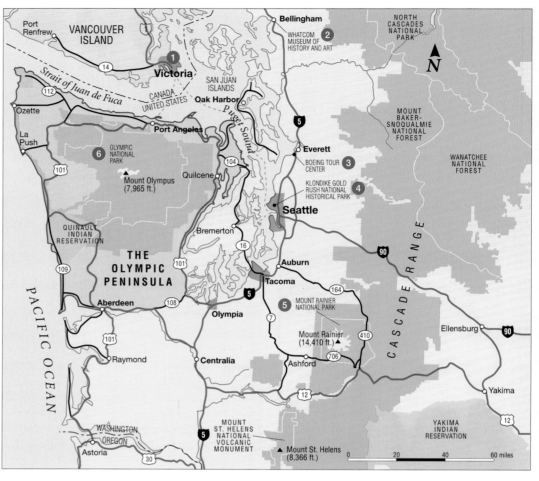

Visitors are dwarfed by the moss-draped giants of Olympic National Park's virgin rain forest. This awe-inspiring display includes Douglas fir, western hemlock, Sitka spruce, and western red cedar.

① VICTORIA, BRITISH COLUMBIA

The picturesque capital of the province of British Columbia is located on the southern tip of Vancouver Island. The city still retains the flavor of its British heritage, harking back to the days when the Royal Navy patrolled the Strait of Juan de Fuca. The Empress Hotel, built in 1908, epitomizes the British influence; the ceremony of taking afternoon tea here is a popular event. Among the city's other attractions are the lush Butchart Gardens, the ornate Parliament Buildings with their green copper domes, the harbor promenade, and the Emily Carr Gallery. British Columbia's seafaring history is explored at the Maritime Museum, while the British Columbia Provincial Museum exhibits artifacts of the Haida, Kwakiutl, and Tsimshian Native peoples. Nearby Thunderbird Park offers a treasure trove of hand-carved totem poles. Located on Hwy. 1.

② WHATCOM MUSEUM OF HISTORY AND ART

Perched on a bluff overlooking Bellingham Bay, the main museum building is housed in an 1892 Victorian structure decked out with cupolas and a clock tower, which once served as Bellingham's city hall. Three other buildings complete the museum complex: an exhibition hall, an education center, and a children's museum. The permanent collection

focuses on the history of the Pacific Northwest. On exhibit are important collections of Northwest Coast Indian artifacts, women's clothing from 1860 to 1910, Victorian dolls and toy furniture, and woodworking tools. Regional history and American art are explored in changing exhibits. Located at 121 Prospect St. in Bellingham.

③ BOEING TOUR CENTER

Tours of the Boeing aircraft plant, located outside Everett, reveal the complex processes and myriad components that go into the manufacture of a modern commercial airliner. The Boeing Company manufactures several hundred airplanes a year, some of which require 6 million parts and 175 miles of wire. The assembly of a Boeing airplane requires a lot of space: the doors of the assembly plant are approximately the size of a football field. By volume, the plant is the largest building in the world, totaling 492 million cubic feet. The building covers 98.36 acres, and many employees use bicycles to get around the facility. The amount of electricity required to light the building could illuminate 32,000 American homes for the same amount of time. Tours begin with a film about the company and the assembly of a modern commercial airliner. Visitors then ride a bus to the assembly building, where they can watch the final assembly of the airplanes. There is also a bus ride to the flight line, where visitors learn about the painting process and see the planes in their final stages before delivery. Located on Hwy. 526, 3 miles west of Hwy. 5.

④ KLONDIKE GOLD RUSH NATIONAL HISTORICAL PARK

During the rush to the Klondike goldfields in 1897, thousands of hopeful prospectors swarmed through Seattle, buying a year's worth of supplies and embarking on ships bound for Skagway, Alaska—the gateway to the Klondike. Today the Seattle segment of Klondike Gold Rush National Historical Park centers on Pioneer Square, which covers 25 city blocks. The area's restored Victorian buildings, built in the Romanesque style, once served as restaurants, outfitters' stores, brothels, and hotels during the gold-rush days. The park's interpretive center shows films about the event and presents exhibits of memorabilia. Nearby at the Seattle Waterfront Park, visitors can stroll along the piers where the steamer *Portland* set out for Alaska carrying the first fortune hunters. Located in downtown Seattle.

⑤ MOUNT RAINIER NATIONAL PARK

A massive dormant volcano, Mount Rainier soars to a height of 14,411 feet, making it the highest peak in the Cascade Range and the most prominent feature of this 235,404-acre national park. Its slopes are blanketed with 25 major glaciers—the largest single-peak glacial system in the contiguous United States. In summer, the mountain's alpine slopes are carpeted with colorful wildflowers, ferns, and mosses.

The snowcapped peaks of the Cascade Range are dominated by Mount Rainier, above, which is visible on the horizon from a distance of 100 miles.

Dense forests of hemlock, red cedar, and Douglas fir grow at lower elevations. Many of these trees are 250 feet high and more than 500 years old. Eighty miles of paved roads lead through the park, taking visitors to Sunrise—the highest point in the park accessible by road—as well as to Paradise, a subalpine meadow dotted with wildflowers. The park's 300 miles of hiking trails include the popular but physically demanding 93-mile-long Wonderland Trail, which circles the mountain. Located 6 miles east of Ashford on Hwy. 706.

⑥ OLYMPIC NATIONAL PARK

The centerpiece of this 922,650-acre national park is 7,965-foot-high Mount Olympus—the highest peak in the Olympic Range. This rugged landscape of towering, snowcapped mountains is the habitat of black-tailed deer, Roosevelt elks, black bears, and marmots. Visitors flock to the park to see the Olympic rain forest—one of only three areas of temperate rain forest in the world. Fed by approximately 150 inches of annual rainfall, the rain forest harbors giant specimens of Douglas fir, western hemlock, Sitka spruce, and western red cedar. The mile-long Hall of Mosses Trail, which starts at the Hoh Visitor Center, allows visitors to see these ancient trees. Olympic National Park's 57-mile-long undeveloped coastal strip beckons visitors to stroll its sandy beaches; at low tide its tidepools offer a miniature wonderland of sea creatures. Offshore, rocky islands called sea stacks dot the coastline. Because of its unspoiled splendor, the United Nations has declared Olympic National Park an International Biosphere Reserve and a World Heritage Site. The main visitor center and entrance to the park are located in Port Angeles on Hwy. 101.

The totem pole, left, is part of a splendid collection on view in Victoria's Thunderbird Park.

KAUAI

*Hawaii's Garden Isle combines
botanical wonders with one of the
world's most spectacular coasts.*

From the flaring peacock hues of the tropical
Pacific, the island of Kauai rises like a green
mirage. Its mountain ramparts are veiled in mist
and often crowned with multiple rainbows. Oldest
of the eight major Hawaiian islands and lushest of
the chain's 132 isles, Kauai was born more than
5 million years ago in the sunless violet depths of
the sea—nearly three miles down—when a fissure opened in the ocean floor, giving birth to a
mighty volcano.

Almost completely round in shape, from the
air Kauai looks like a limpet—a sea creature wedded to the rocks of the land. The volcano that
formed the island ranks as the largest shield volcano in the Hawaiian archipelago, with a volume
of 1,000 cubic miles. At the volcano's summit
yawns a crater 13 miles across.

Kauai's sister island, the privately owned
Niihau, nestles off its southwestern shore. Lower,
drier, smaller, and in the lee of Kauai's splendor,
Niihau was born of the same volcanic fires. Over
the years, as siblings sometimes do, Niihau and
Kauai drifted apart. The channel between the
islands became wider, but never very deep.

Kauai's landscapes are as spectacular as they are varied. There are tropical arboretums where flowers explode with brilliant color; dry desert gardens bearing blossoms bravely on their wind-twisted limbs; highland marsh where the dew settles on delicate petals; deep canyons where vegetation sprouts determinedly from the volcanic rock; and sunny beach parks that are shaded by coconut palms and scattered with hau blooms. Because of its abundant plant life, Kauai is known as the Garden Isle.

The island owes this great fertility to its volcanic beginnings. Kauai was formed when volcanic fires spewed out molten lava, pushing up vast mounds, pillows, and basaltic boulders. The island, whose center is named Waialeale—meaning "a rippling upon the waters"—rose above the waves to continue its fiery growth. No human saw this giant mountain of fire or the pillars of steam announcing its arrival. Winds, storms, earthquakes, tides, and time tore and chiseled the volcano into ragged, wild, and magnificently sculpted mountain ranges, valleys, coastal plains, towering sea cliffs, and the Pacific's most awesome canyon—Waimea.

It is difficult for a visitor to imagine how Kauai looked when it emerged from the Pacific. The new island was ashen, sterile, and still smoldering. As Waialeale stretched higher, it snagged the fleets of downy clouds that sail above the southern seas and drew precious cooling rain to its slopes. Life came slowly, as seeds were deposited by ocean currents, winds, and migratory birds. It took about 40,000 years for each new plant species to take hold. In isolation, these castaways evolved into a range of flora and fauna not found anywhere else on the planet. Fifteen ancestor bird species, for instance, in time became 70 unique native species, each singing its own psalm of life. There were also a few no-shows on this oceanic ark: Kauai has no native reptiles or amphibians and only two mammals—the bat and the seal.

BOTANICAL BOUNTY

The Garden Isle abounds in botanical gardens and nature preserves. Every home has a front-yard garden where house plants grow as big as the houses themselves, and mango, banana, papaya, litchi, and guava trees are heavy with gifts of fruit.

Queen Emma, widow of King Kamehameha IV, selected Kauai when she planted her famed garden during the 1870's. It was later expanded, and then chartered by Congress in 1964 as the National Tropical Botanical Garden. Set among glades and streams at Lawai, Queen Emma's garden includes more than 6,000 species of plants.

All this bounty is nurtured by Old Waialeale. At 5,148 feet in height, the mountain is one of the wettest spots on earth, receiving in excess of 400 inches of rain a year. The winds at the top can blow a person down, and the fog is so thick that visibility can drop to an arm's length. Ohia trees, which tower as high as 80 feet, hug the ground like natural bonsai, sending out scarlet blossoms on two-inch branches to brighten the primordial gloom.

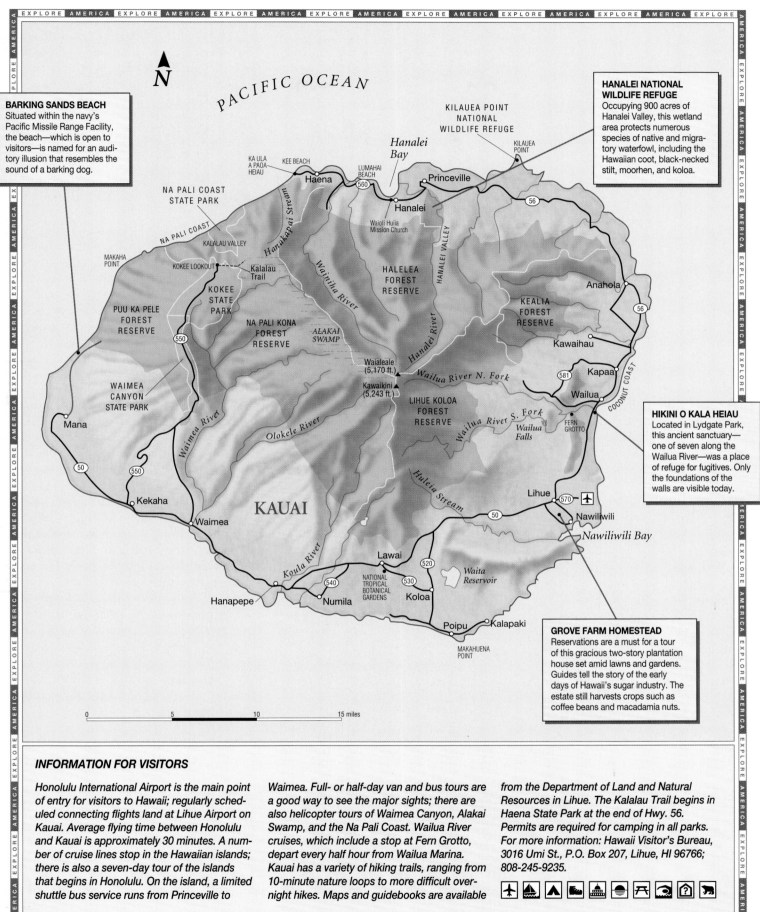

BARKING SANDS BEACH
Situated within the navy's Pacific Missile Range Facility, the beach—which is open to visitors—is named for an auditory illusion that resembles the sound of a barking dog.

HANALEI NATIONAL WILDLIFE REFUGE
Occupying 900 acres of Hanalei Valley, this wetland area protects numerous species of native and migratory waterfowl, including the Hawaiian coot, black-necked stilt, moorhen, and koloa.

HIKINI O KALA HEIAU
Located in Lydgate Park, this ancient sanctuary—one of seven along the Wailua River—was a place of refuge for fugitives. Only the foundations of the walls are visible today.

GROVE FARM HOMESTEAD
Reservations are a must for a tour of this gracious two-story plantation house set amid lawns and gardens. Guides tell the story of the early days of Hawaii's sugar industry. The estate still harvests crops such as coffee beans and macadamia nuts.

PACIFIC OCEAN

KILAUEA POINT NATIONAL WILDLIFE REFUGE

KILAUEA POINT

Hanalei Bay

KA ULA A PAOA HEIAU

KEE BEACH

LUMAHAI BEACH

Haena

Princeville

560

Hanalei

56

Waioli Huiia Mission Church

NA PALI COAST STATE PARK

NA PALI COAST

KALALAU VALLEY

Hanakapiai Stream

HALELEA FOREST RESERVE

HANALEI VALLEY

Anahola

56

MAKAHA POINT

KOKEE LOOKOUT

Kalalau Trail

KOKEE STATE PARK

Waintha River

Hanalei River

KEALIA FOREST RESERVE

Kawaihau

PUU KA PELE FOREST RESERVE

NA PALI KONA FOREST RESERVE

ALAKAI SWAMP

550

581

Kapaa

COCONUT COAST

Waialeale (5,170 ft.)

Wailua River N. Fork

Wailua

WAIMEA CANYON STATE PARK

Kawaikini (5,243 ft.)

LIHUE KOLOA FOREST RESERVE

Wailua River S. Fork

FERN GROTTO

Wailua Falls

Mana

Olokele River

Waimea River

50

550

HIKINI O KALA HEIAU

Kekaha

Waimea

Koula River

Huleia Stream

Lihue

570

KAUAI

Nawiliwili

50

Nawiliwili Bay

Lawai

520

Waita Reservoir

Hanapepe

540

Numila

530

NATIONAL TROPICAL BOTANICAL GARDENS

Koloa

Kalapaki

Poipu

MAKAHUENA POINT

N

0   5   10   15 miles

INFORMATION FOR VISITORS

Honolulu International Airport is the main point of entry for visitors to Hawaii; regularly scheduled connecting flights land at Lihue Airport on Kauai. Average flying time between Honolulu and Kauai is approximately 30 minutes. A number of cruise lines stop in the Hawaiian islands; there is also a seven-day tour of the islands that begins in Honolulu. On the island, a limited shuttle bus service runs from Princeville to Waimea. Full- or half-day van and bus tours are a good way to see the major sights; there are also helicopter tours of Waimea Canyon, Alakai Swamp, and the Na Pali Coast. Wailua River cruises, which include a stop at Fern Grotto, depart every half hour from Wailua Marina. Kauai has a variety of hiking trails, ranging from 10-minute nature loops to more difficult overnight hikes. Maps and guidebooks are available from the Department of Land and Natural Resources in Lihue. The Kalalau Trail begins in Haena State Park at the end of Hwy. 56. Permits are required for camping in all parks. For more information: Hawaii Visitor's Bureau, 3016 Umi St., P.O. Box 207, Lihue, HI 96766; 808-245-9235.

Waialeale's emerald-green crater streams with hundreds of waterfalls. The vast Alakai Swamp, the watershed that fills the rivers of the island, oozes from the western flank of the mountain. Its rushing waters bring life to the dry sunny coastlands, replenishing the gardens and the fields of sugarcane, fruit, coffee, and taro, along with Kauai's numerous golf courses.

Taro is one of Kauai's most aesthetically pleasing crops, as well as being the Hawaiian dietary staple. Taro leaves taste like spinach, and its corm (or bulb) is baked, pounded into poi, or fried up as taro chips. From the overlook at Princeville, the lush *lo'i* (water-filled taro patches) that carpet the Hanalei Valley glisten at the feet of towering mountains. From the lookout, visitors are awed by magnificent vistas of the green valley, the Hanalei River, and the ocean.

The Na Pali Coast is truly a place of dramatic beauty. This rugged volcanic fortress of sheer verdant mountains is notched with deep valleys and besieged by cobalt waves that turn foaming white as they hurl themselves ashore. There are eerie sea caves eroded into the cliffs along the shoreline and towering cascades that plunge, wind-whipped and singing, hundreds of feet into the surf.

No road has tamed the wilderness of the coast. The area is approachable by boat in summer when the surf is low; by helicopter, or by foot along the 11-mile Kalalau Trail, which hugs the palisades. The trail snakes into valleys and dips under waterfalls, rising and falling with the contours of the land. A thousand feet above the waves, the land trembles with the impact of the ocean as its waters continue to sculpt the Na Pali Coast.

All the wild and lonely valleys found along the Na Pali Coast—Limahuli, Hanakapiai, Hoolulu, Waiahuakua, Nualolo, Milolii, Awaawapuhi, Honopu, Hanakoa, and Kalalau—were once inhabited. There are tales of lost tribes, giant lizards, and little Menehune people who worked only by moonlight. Kings and commoners fished and farmed, loved, begat, and died in this remote and formidable wilderness, with sunsets that sear the soul and a natural bounty that exceeds the wildest expectations. Shrouded by time and hidden within the jungle are the remains of agricultural terraces, temples, dwellings, and burial caves. The Kalalau Trail is still paved in places with the stones laid down by some of the coast's earliest inhabitants.

A view of the Na Pali Coast and Kalalau Valley can be gleaned from the 4,000-foot lookout at Kokee State Park. Hiking trails and nature walks abound in the park, some descending into Kalalau, others skirting the ridges. There are cabins, a lodge with a restaurant, and the remarkable Kokee Museum, with exhibits on the fascinating natural history of the island.

WAIMEA CANYON

The road to the lookout begins at Waimea, where British explorer Capt. James Cook first landed on the Hawaiian Islands on January 19, 1778. A statue of Cook stands in the main street of the town. As the road to Kokee winds upward, it skirts the lip of Waimea Canyon. Called the Grand Canyon of the Pacific, it runs 2,000 feet deep and spreads out as far as the eye can behold. Gouged out by the rains flowing from Waialeale, the canyon glows in shades of umber, amber, ocher, celadon, and lavender. Here

Kauai's bare bones are laid out, exposing the roseate layers of lava that built the island.

In ancient times, the most desirable place to live on Kauai was the fertile land at the mouth of the Wailua River, which was reserved as the domain of the chiefs and priests. The river region became known as far away as Tahiti as Wailua Nui Hoana, meaning "Great Sacred Wailua." Tour boats on the Wailua take visitors upstream to Fern Grotto, while musicians and hula dancers perform tales of river life. At the fern-lipped cavern, the musicians sing the traditional "Hawaiian Wedding Song," urging couples to hold hands, repeat vows, and profess their love. Kayakers can explore the south fork of the Wailua, which trickles from the very heart of the island.

Kauai jealously guards its pristine beauty. More than 90 percent of the island is virtually inaccessible by road. Residents, businesses, and hotels all participate in wildlife conservation programs, especially those aimed at preserving bird habitats and migratory routes. The kolea, or golden plover, flies more than 2,000 miles to winter on Kauai, settling in with the boobies and the native nene—Hawaii's

official state bird—at the Kilauea Point National Wildlife Refuge.

It is an accepted custom that no building on Kauai may be taller than a coconut palm. Tourism is confined to several distinct enclaves, where the hotels are almost overrun by the flora. Princeville, a resort town on the North Shore, features 11,000 acres of manicured luxury and three championship golf courses. The Coconut Coast contains small hotels and tiny towns along the shore from Wailua to Kapaa. Poipu is the principal tourist center in the dry and sunny south; just down the beach to the east is Kalapaki, with lagoons and the biggest swimming pool in the state.

Most of Kauai, however, remains determinedly rural. Fields of sugarcane wave in the trade winds; cattle and even buffalo roam the open range areas. The towns are so small that dogs doze in the roads, but the streets harbor contemporary surprises.

Sleepy Hanapepe has a number of noteworthy art galleries. Waimea is crammed with little stores and a hotel that consists of refurbished plantation cottages. The old wooden storefronts of Koloa, a former sugar town near Poipu, have been renovated and outfitted as boutiques and restaurants. Lihue, the county seat, is big enough for a couple of traffic lights, but not big enough for pretension.

THE LITTLE PEOPLE

The first Hawaiians came to Kauai from the Marquesas archipelago and Tahiti. A commonly accepted date for their arrival is A.D. 1000, although recent archeological evidence suggests it may have been earlier. It is said that these migrants found a race of small people living on Kauai known as the Menehune. Called the leprechauns of the Pacific, they were thought to perform mischievous acts by stealth of night. Such

RECENT ARRIVAL
Kauai is rich in native plant species, but the purple bougainvillea from South America, above, was introduced to Hawaii only in the late 1800's.

JOYFUL WATERS
Amid palms and tropical plants, the Waioli Huiia Mission Church outside Hanalei, below, preserves a touch of New England. Waioli means "joyful waters" and was named for a local waterfall. The mission was established in 1834 by Rev. William P. Alexander; the Mission House is now a museum furnished in Victorian style.

credence is given the myth that *manahune* is today a derisive Tahitian word for commoner.

Kauai was never conquered by Hawaii's warrior king, Kamehameha the Great. In 1810, however, he voluntarily joined his kingdom, uniting the Hawaiian islands for the first time in history.

The island's sense of *lokahi*—"unity"—came to the fore in 1992, when Hurricane Iniki destroyed or damaged 70 percent of Kauai's homes and stripped the gardens and forests. Residents, working with nature, quickly restored the island to its splendor, as celebrated in an old Hawaiian chant:

Beautiful is Kauai beyond compare,
She sends forth a bud in the summit of Waialeale,
She flowers in the heights of Kawaikini,
Her strength radiates in awful splendor from the
    Alakai;
Though I weary, though I faint, she renews my
    strength in her soft petals.

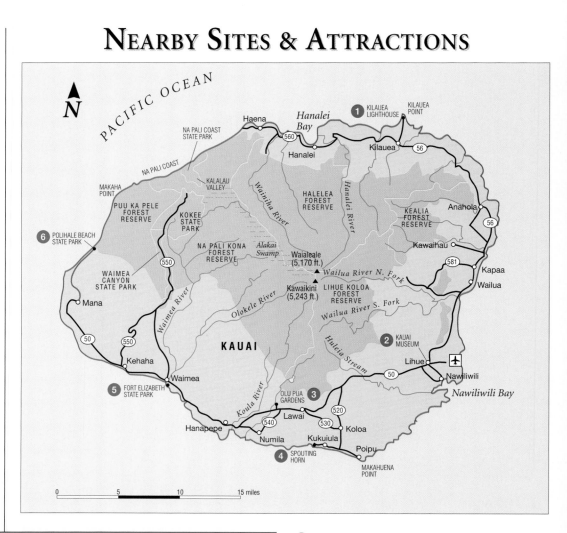

Kilauea Lighthouse lies on a rugged narrow peninsula within Kilauea National Wildlife Refuge.

1 KILAUEA LIGHTHOUSE

Constructed in 1913, this national historic landmark is located at the tip of Kilauea Point, within the Kilauea National Wildlife Refuge. The lighthouse once boasted the largest clam-shaped lens in the world. The lens was retired from service in the 1970's, when it was replaced by a smaller, high-density light. Today the navigation beacon of Kilauea can be seen from as far away as 90 miles out to sea. The rocky coastline of the wildlife refuge is a popular nesting ground for birds such as wedge-tailed shearwaters, red-footed boobies, and great frigates, which are often seen soaring above the cliffs. Hawaiian monk seals, green turtles, dolphins, and humpback whales can be spotted offshore. A visitor center provides information on the flora and fauna of the area and also traces the history of the lighthouse. Located 5 miles north of the town of Kilauea on Kilauea Rd.

2 KAUAI MUSEUM

The two buildings of this small museum contain a fine collection of Hawaiian artifacts, including feather leis, calabashes, Hawaiian quilts, a hand-carved canoe, stone tools, a four-poster bed made of koa wood, and native bowls. The Senda Gallery displays early 20th-century photographs of the island, and the William Hyde Rice Building focuses on the natural history and cultural heritage of Kauai. One of the

highlights of the Rice Building is a unique collection of seashells from around the world. Also on display is an exhibit of rare photographs of Kauai's nearest neighbor, the privately owned island of Niihau. Other museum exhibits include a scale model replica of a traditional Hawaiian village, an extensive collection of Hawaiian weapons, and a video presentation that provides visitors with a simulated aerial tour of the island. The museum also houses a model of Capt. James Cook's ship H.M.S. *Resolution*, as well as logbook excerpts from the day in 1778 when the great seafarer discovered the Hawaiian islands. Located at 4428 Rice St. in Lihue.

🏛️ 🏠

③ OLU PUA GARDENS

Macadamia trees line the road to these sprawling 12.5-acre gardens on the grounds of the Alexander Pineapple Plantation. The gardens are divided into four distinct zones: the Kau Kau Garden is devoted to fruit trees and edible plants; the Hibiscus Garden features displays of Hawaii's state flower; the Palm Garden contains a lush tropical forest of palm trees; and the Jungle Garden flourishes with tropical flowers, plants, and trees, including vanilla orchids, Hong Kong orchids, heliconias, and ginger. Guided tours of the gardens also allow visitors to see the exterior of the main plantation house, designed in the 1930's by the prominent Honolulu architect C. W. Dickey. Located ½ mile north of Lawai on Hwy. 50.

🅖 🏠 👣

④ SPOUTING HORN

This geological oddity consists of a half-submerged lava tube, created when molten lava cooled and hardened on the outside. Nowadays, when conditions are right, the tube fills with water and spews a column of water 50 feet into the air through a blowhole. This generates a loud sound similar to that of a whale expelling air. Hawaiian legend attributes the howling sound to a melancholy lizard who swam from Niihau to Kauai. Mourning the loss of his sisters, the lizard's tear-filled eyes are said to have caused him to overshoot the beach and land in the blowhole, where he is trapped forever. Years ago local farmers, upset at the amount of salty spray that the fountain deposited on their sugarcane fields, increased the size of the blowhole in order to decrease its power. Located 4 miles southwest of Koloa on Hwy. 530.

🏛️ 🌅

⑤ FORT ELIZABETH STATE PARK

Yellow ilima flowers cover the walls of Fort Elizabeth, one of three forts built at the behest of German adventurer Georg Anton Schaeffer. Posing as an agent of the Russian American Company of Alaska, Schaeffer convinced Hawaiian King Kamualii that the fort was necessary to protect Russian trading interests. Within a year, Schaeffer was exposed as a fraud and forced to leave Hawaii, but Fort Elizabeth was nevertheless completed in 1817 and manned by Hawaiian troops until 1864. A staircase brings visitors to the top of the battlements, where 38 cannons still have their sights aimed at picturesque Waimea Bay. The fort's elevated position provides a

panoramic view of the surrounding landscape. Located ½ mile east of Waimea on Hwy. 50.

🚫 🏛️ 🌅 🏕️

⑥ POLIHALE BEACH STATE PARK

Stretching along the northwest coast of Kauai, the white sand of Polihale Beach is popular with sun worshipers. Dunes are dotted with reddish-yellow blooms of ohai bushes and white-berried, white-petaled beach naupakas, whose half flowers, which grow on only one side of the plants, are a legendary symbol of separated lovers' broken hearts. The beach is known for its spectacular sunsets and its views of the islands of Niihau and Lehua. According to Hawaiian folklore, the park contains an area where the spirits of the dead depart. (*Polihale* is a Hawaiian word meaning "saved in one's bosom.") Located 7 miles north of Mana on an unpaved road.

🏖️ 🏛️ 🌅 🏕️ 🤿

Recognizable by their white half flowers, white berries, and curled, waxy leaves, beach naupaka plants dot the rippling sand at Polihale Beach State Park.

As water and air are sucked into a tube of hardened lava, Spouting Horn provides a spectacular display, discharging a giant column of water into the air.

Merritt Island, Florida

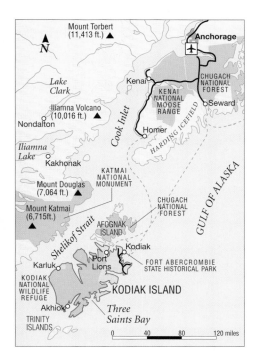

Wildflowers soften the wave-lashed coastline of Fort Abercrombie State Historical Park, located in the northeastern corner of Kodiak Island.

A s seen from the window of an airplane headed south from Anchorage, an emerald land of Sitka spruce forest and snowcapped mountains emerges from the Gulf of Alaska. This glimmering jewel is Kodiak Island, where the world's biggest grizzly bear prowls the rugged terrain, and a small human population maintains one of America's largest fishing fleets.

The 3,588-square-mile island is notched by so many inlets that no part of it is very far from tidewater. Multitudes of sea otters and sea lions once provided food and warmth for the island's 8,000-year-old Koniag and Aleut cultures. In 1794 this profusion of sea mammals drew Russian fur trader Grigor Shelikof to the island. Shelikof subdued the Koniag people and set up camp in Three Saints Bay. In 1792 Alexander Baranov moved the settlement to the present-day site of the city of Kodiak on the northeastern side of the island.

In Kodiak, a two-story log warehouse built by Baranov for storing sea otter pelts now houses the Baranov Museum's collection of Russian samovars, icons, and trade beads, as well as bone and stone tools from the Koniag era. At the Alutiiq Cultural Center, highlights include a spruce-framed kayak that was used by the Aleut for hunting marine mammals and a diorama of a prehistoric Koniag village.

The Russian Orthodox church plays an integral role in the life of the tightly knit community. Stouthearted citizens reconstructed the town in the wake of the 1912 eruption of Mount Katmai, only to have to rebuild it again after a 1964 earthquake and tidal wave destroyed Kodiak.

FISHING HAVEN

In the late 1800's, salmon were so plentiful that islanders joked it was possible to walk across local streams on the backs of the fish. A century later sport fishermen still feast on five species of salmon: pink, chinook, chum, sockeye, and silver. Anglers can hook grayling and giant halibut just minutes from the dock, or venture to Kodiak's rivers for catches of steelhead, rainbow trout, Dolly Varden, and Arctic char.

Some Kodiak guests come just for the bears. The massive beasts sit hunched over streams, waiting to dig their claws into plump salmon. Set up to protect the Kodiak brown bear, Kodiak National Wildlife Refuge occupies about two-thirds of the island. Among the refuge's dense thickets of willow, alder, and elderberry live native red foxes, river otters, short-tailed weasels, tundra voles, and brown bats. Non-native wildlife includes Sitka black-tailed deer, mountain goats, snowshoe hares, Arctic ground squirrels, and beavers.

Motorists reach the end of Kodiak's road system at Fossil Beach. Searching for fossil shells among the clay and rocks, beachcombers can look up and see gray whales swimming past on their fall journey to California. Strolling along the pristine shores, visitors soon realize that not all island paradises are in the tropics.

FOR MORE INFORMATION:
Alaska Division of Tourism, P.O. Box 110801, Juneau, AK 99811-0801; 907-465-2010.

The blue onion domes of the Holy Resurrection Orthodox Church recall Kodiak's Russian heritage. The interior of the church is adorned with radiantly colored icons.

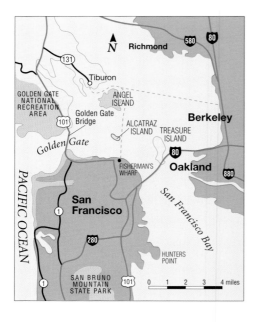

Treacherous currents and chilly waters were a powerful deterrent to would-be escapees from Alcatraz. The island's position in San Francisco Bay made it an ideal location for a maximum-security prison.

I n the middle of San Francisco Bay looms a huge mass of sandstone that is often shrouded in dense fog. The bleak island is Alcatraz, formerly America's toughest federal prison. Nowadays tourists line up for ferry rides from Fisherman's Wharf to the island, but the 1,500 inmates held during the prison's history thought only of escaping "the tomb of the living dead."

Known as The Rock, the island housed a prison designed to inspire awe and fear in Depression-era gangsters. With an officer-to-inmate ratio averaging one to five, the detention center was a limited-privilege, maximum-security prison, where meal-times lasted just 20 minutes and inmates showered only twice weekly.

OFFSHORE ATTRACTION
Alcatraz was designated a federal penitentiary in 1934, but the 12-acre rock's penal history goes back to Civil War days, when the island served as a fortress. Named an official U.S. military prison in 1861, the facility was transferred to the federal Bureau of Prisons in 1933. Alcatraz was finally closed in 1963, only to be occupied by Native American protesters in 1969-70.

Now open to the public as part of Golden Gate National Recreation Area, Alcatraz is accessible by ferry from San Francisco's Pier 41. Visitors disembark at the dock where Al Capone and "Machine Gun" Kelly first stepped ashore. Agave Trail leads up a stone stairway to the parade ground, where a towering lighthouse and the sprawling prison dominate the scene. Visitors can learn about famous escapes and take the Cellhouse Tour, guided by a rented cassette featuring sound effects and interviews with former inmates and guards.

Cellblock A has survived virtually unaltered from the days when Alcatraz served as a U.S. military prison.

Inside the prison, the menu of the last meal served at Alcatraz is still posted. Six of the cells in D Block—the special disciplinary unit—have thick, 250-pound steel doors, which totally close out daylight. One of D Block's 36 isolation chambers—cell 42—was for six years the home of Robert Stroud, better known as the Birdman of Alcatraz, who earned his nickname by studying bird diseases during his internment at Leavenworth prison in Kansas.

Alcatraz itself was named in 1775 by the Spaniard Juan Manuel de Ayala, who christened it Isla de los Alcatraces ("island of the pelicans"). Part of the island is reclaimed by birds from mid-February to late August, when Agave Trail is closed to visitors in order to protect western gulls and black-crowned night-herons. Studded with 20-foot-high agave plants, the trail's lush vegetation softens the harshness of The Rock. Benches nestled among cypress trees and sweet alyssum look out over the steel blue waters of San Francisco Bay. Beholding the magnificent skyline, visitors realize that the worst punishment on Alcatraz was neither the rigid rules nor solitary confinement, but rather the view of breezy San Francisco—agonizingly near, yet so far away.

FOR MORE INFORMATION:
Red and White Fleet, Pier 41, Fisherman's Wharf, San Francisco, CA 94133; 415-546-2700.

Jutting into the Pacific Ocean, the hooked triangle of Point Reyes Peninsula looks as if it might split off and drift into the sea at any time. At Point Reyes, rupturing and buckling along the San Andreas Fault has given rise to an eclectic mix of scenery. Threaded with 140 miles of hiking and cycling trails, this national seashore covers 100 square miles of contrasting terrain.

On the Earthquake Trail in Bear Valley, visitors can straddle the San Andreas Fault and learn about the 1906 San Francisco earthquake, when the peninsula jumped almost 20 feet northwest in relation to the rest of the continent. Windswept Point Reyes is still moving northwest at a rate of two inches per year. Olema Valley Trail leads to another fault phenomenon: located only a few hundred feet apart, Olema Creek and Pine Gulch Creek are parallel, yet flow in opposite directions.

DRAKE'S LANDFALL

English adventurer Sir Francis Drake was the first European to explore the peninsula. Drakes Bay is believed to be the beach where Drake grounded his ship, *Golden Hind*, for repairs in 1579, before resuming his round-the-world voyage. Light shale cliffs rise 200 feet above Drakes Bay, where swimmers enjoy dark blue waters sheltered from the stealthy undertow and bullying riptides of the peninsula's northern points.

Just around the bend from Drakes Bay, gray whales swim past lookouts on Chimney Rock Trail during their yearly journey to and from Alaska. Nearby Sea Lion Overlook is a prime site for spotting sea lions basking on offshore rocks.

Thick mists often cloak the 1870 Point Reyes Lighthouse, where winds sometimes reach 130 miles an hour. Brown pelicans, black oystercatchers, and the occasional tufted puffin patrol the lighthouse rocks and cliff areas. But the best bird-watching in the peninsula is along Estero Trail, which winds through salt marshes populated with cormorants, great blue herons, and egrets. At the southern end of the peninsula, interested visitors can observe bird banding at the Point Reyes Bird Observatory—the only full-time ornithological field research station on the continent. Turkey vultures soar above Inverness Ridge, the granite backbone of the peninsula. Hikers can trek up 1,407-foot Mount Wittenberg, the ridge's highest point, or stay overnight at one of four campgrounds.

Tomales Point Trail offers visitors the opportunity to spot tule elk. A refuge was created here for the species, which had been reduced to only one pair in 1875. The area blooms with orange California poppy, blue lupine, and yellow mustard.

Point Reyes has changed little since the coastal Miwok Indians hunted deer and elk in the forest, caught salmon in the Pacific Ocean, and gathered shellfish along the shore. Kule Loklo, a reconstructed Miwok village near Bear Valley Visitor Center, describes how the peaceful Miwoks lived harmoniously in Point Reyes' many different environments for 1,000 years before the arrival of Europeans.

FOR MORE INFORMATION:
Superintendent, Point Reyes National Seashore, Point Reyes, CA 94956; 415-663-1092.

Erosion has sculpted the cliffs at Drakes Bay into softly undulating forms. It was near here that Sir Francis Drake made landfall, christening Point Reyes Nova Albion.

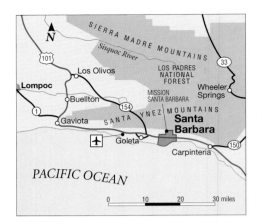

Nestled at the base of the Santa Ynez Mountains approximately 90 miles west of Los Angeles, the mission town of Santa Barbara became a popular seaside resort in the late 1800's, when construction of the Southern Pacific Railroad brought visitors to the town's renowned mineral springs. Today Santa Barbara's downtown district evokes the town's Spanish heritage: streets bearing Spanish names are lined with whitewashed, red-roofed buildings reminiscent of Spanish villas and Moorish architecture. The town's rich past is further displayed in its historic mission-style adobe dwellings, bell towers, museums, and the famed Mission Santa Barbara.

Santa Barbara traces its history back to 1602, when Spanish conquistador Sebastian Vizcaino sailed into Santa Barbara Bay and christened the area in honor of the saint who was born on that date. Almost two centuries later, in 1782, mission founder Father Junípero Serra arrived in Santa Barbara accompanied by a military contingent. Serra's expedition first established a presidio, where the city now stands. Four years later he built Santa Barbara's famous mission on the hills above the fledgling settlement. It was the tenth of the 21 Franciscan missions to be built by the Spanish in California.

Santa Barbara's wealth of terra-cotta roofs and Spanish Revival buildings are the result of a mandatory building code that ensured that the city would retain its Spanish character after a 1925 earthquake forced the reconstruction of much of the city. The Red Tile Tour guides strollers on a 12-block journey through the center of Santa Barbara, where bougainvillea cascade down whitewashed walls and street corners are punctuated with fir trees. Also featured in the tour is El Presidio de Santa Barbara State Historic Park. The park's historic highlight includes El Cuartel ("the barracks"), a tiny two-room adobe structure built in 1782, which is the sole vestige of the original presidio, as well as the oldest building in the city. The park also contains adobe homes and a reconstructed adobe chapel.

On the grounds of the Santa Barbara Historical Society Museum, a historic adobe structure that was built in 1836 lies adjacent to the L-shaped 1817 Covarrubias Adobe, where the last Mexican Congress in California may have met in 1846. The museum building is the home of diverse displays that range from Chumash Indian artifacts, Mexican ranchers' implements, and Yankee traders' items to antique Victorian dolls and costumes. Of special interest is a magnificent gold-leaf Chinese shrine, once belonging to the Chee Kung Tong, a secret political society that existed at the turn of the century.

Casa de la Guerra, an 1828 U-shaped adobe structure, was once the home of a presidio commander and now forms part of a Spanish-style cobbled shopping arcade called El Paseo. Walkers can stop at an outdoor cafe by the courtyard's fountain. The clock tower that adorns the 1929 county courthouse affords spectacular views of tiled roofs and palm-lined avenues. With its sculptured facade and sunken gardens, the palatial courthouse epitomizes Spanish-style architecture. On the second floor, murals depict important local events.

SEASIDE SOJOURN

The city's main thoroughfare, State Street, leads to Stearns Wharf and to oceanside Cabrillo Boulevard, where local artisans display their crafts every Sunday. Built in 1872, Stearns Wharf is California's oldest working pier. The three-block-long wharf is a bustling place where visitors can sample vintages from local wineries, board whale-watching boats, and watch fishermen unload their catches.

Santa Barbara's gently curving beaches are sprinkled with picnic tables and volleyball nets. A three-mile-long waterfront path is an invitation to skaters, cyclists, and joggers, while the clear blue waters of the ocean attract surfers, snorkelers, and swimmers. Nestled in the crook of the breakwater to the west side of Stearns Wharf, a 92-acre yacht harbor shelters the local fishing fleet, along with hundreds of pleasure craft. From a charter boat, divers can explore nearby kelp beds and underwater pinnacles that are covered with multicol-

Santa Barbara's Spanish-style architecture is a byword for elegance. Municipal ordinances and preservation-minded locals ensure that the city retains a Hispanic flavor.

ored anemones. Lucky divers may even encounter a school of dolphins.

The city's most famous landmark—Mission Santa Barbara—is perched on a low ridge of the Santa Ynez Mountains. Built by the Chumash Indians under Spanish direction, the mission was completed in 1820. The sandstone church, with its twin domed masonry towers, is still used for religious services. It is often referred to as the Queen of the Missions because of its beautiful design and elegant gardens. Visitors to the mission can explore the chapel, library, curio room, and kitchens, or linger in the peaceful cemetery under the shade of a giant fig tree. Each May, local artists take part in a lively and colorful festival of sidewalk art.

The Spanish nicknamed the area *la tierra adorada*—"the adored land." While beholding Santa Barbara's eucalyptus-clad hills and its many architectural monuments, modern visitors may fall in love with it, too.

FOR MORE INFORMATION:
Santa Barbara Conference and Visitors Bureau, 510A State St., Santa Barbara, CA 93101; 805-966-9222.

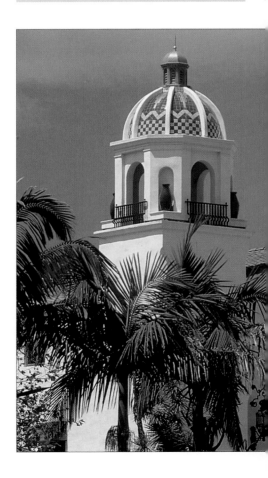

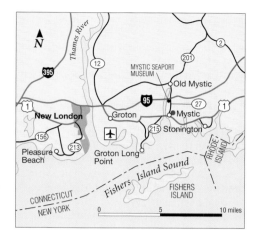

The masts of Mystic Seaport's famed whaling ship Charles W. Morgan *tower above the weathered shingles of a dockside building. The ship takes its name from its first owner, a Quaker merchant.*

Weatherworn mastheads poke through veils of fog as ships' hulls rise and fall with the waves of the Mystic River. Footsteps clatter on stone-paved lanes, mingling with the distant clang of a blacksmith pounding iron. Though more visitors than swashbuckling sailors tread the harbor's granite wharves these days, the sights and sounds of Mystic have changed very little since its shipyards launched the nation's most magnificent vessels more than a century ago.

Settled in the mid-17th century, Mystic quickly became a center for shipbuilders and seafarers alike. From 1838 to 1878, the village's shipyards launched more than 300 vessels, including the clipper *David Crockett*, renowned for its record-breaking voyages around Cape Horn to San Francisco.

Located in Mystic is Mystic Seaport, the Museum of America and the Sea, a 17-acre reconstructed showcase of maritime crafts and nautical lore that re-creates life in an early shipbuilding town. Visitors can observe carvers sculpt figureheads, learn how coopers make barrels, hum along with chantey singers, and see boats being built.

FAMOUS FLEET

Mystic Seaport's fleet is unparalleled to this day. Docked at Chubb's Wharf is the 1841 *Charles W. Morgan*, the sole surviving square-rigged whaling ship in the nation. Landlubbers can explore the main deck and peek into the blubber room and officers' mess of this 113-foot vessel, which carried up to 2,700 barrels of whale oil. Students of Mystic's sailing program live aboard the 1882 Danish-built *Joseph Conrad*, a fully rigged training ship. The *L.A. Dunton*, a classic Gloucester fishing schooner built in 1821, is moored at Hobie's Dock. Here visitors can climb aboard the 1908 steamboat *Sabino*—the last coal-fired passenger ferry operating in the United States—for scenic tours of the Mystic River.

Mystic Seaport's collection of small craft such as smacks, sloops, draggers, and catboats, which date from the 1800's to the 1930's, is the largest in the world. At the museum's preservation shipyard a 375-ton-capacity lift dock, used to haul boats out of the water, is displayed along with dusty carpenters' shops, an 85-foot spar lathe, and a rigging loft strewn with bits of rope.

Visitors can learn about ship construction and design at the Small Boat Shop, where shipyard carpenters faithfully create replicas of historically significant craft and demonstrate boat-building techniques. Close to Chubb's Wharf, the Stillman Building houses relics of seaport life. Tools of coastal fishermen and fans from Asia are displayed among diaries of shorebound captains' wives, scrimshaw (carved from whale ivory), and finely crafted ship models.

Whether enjoying a clam bake, strolling past meticulously restored buildings, watching the art of boat building, or learning about navigation, visitors to Mystic Seaport are transported back to the days when sailing ships ruled the seas.

FOR MORE INFORMATION:
Mystic Seaport, 75 Greenmanville Ave., P.O. Box 600, Mystic, CT 06355-0990; 203-572-0711.

Antique woodcarvers' tools hint at the multiplicity of skills required to build a sailing ship. These tools would likely have been used by the craftsmen who carved ships' figureheads.

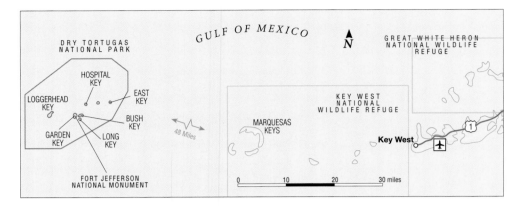

A few miles off the westernmost tip of the Florida Keys, a cluster of small islands forms the Dry Tortugas. The group lies within Dry Tortugas National Park, a 65,000-acre preserve with just 85 acres above water. Once the lair of pirates, these remote isles now harbor snorkelers and divers drawn by unspoiled dive sites. While swimmers frolic in the warm, clear waters, landlubbers revel in watching wildlife and exploring Fort Jefferson, the nation's largest coastal fort.

When Spanish explorer Ponce de Leon arrived in 1513, he named the islands Las Tortugas for the abundant sea turtles that roamed the islands' shores. Because there is no supply of fresh water on the islands, however, later visitors wryly renamed them the Dry Tortugas.

The Dry Tortugas' abundance of natural treasures include the endangered hawksbill, green leatherback, and loggerhead sea turtles. These animals still seek refuge in the keys, feeding on marine invertebrates and aquatic plants. The females excavate their nests on the islands' sandy shores, lay their eggs, and retreat seaward. Hatchlings instinctively head for the waters, but only a few survive a journey filled with predators.

Flocks of sooty terns treat bird-watchers to spectacular displays as they gather by the thousands for nesting season on Bush Key. The islet is closed from March to October to protect the rookery's sandy nests, but nature lovers can view the white-and-black sooties from Garden Key. Nesting in bay cedar and sea lavender, about 2,500 brown noddy terns mingle with the sooties, swooping down to catch fish and squid.

Preying on tern hatchlings, elegant frigate birds with seven-foot wingspans soar above Long Key, while peregrine falcons hover around Loggerhead Key. Other avian species include the roseate tern, double-crested cormorant, brown pelican, and painted bunting. Patient birders may spot masked and brown boobies on Hospital Key.

Under the ocean, Dry Tortugas National Park is a kaleidoscope of multicolored sea fans, rose and purple sea anemones, and reef fish in brash hues of red, yellow, green, and blue. Underwater forests of staghorn coral formations support schools of fish that dart away at the approach of a shark or barracuda. Submerged shipwrecks, some dating to the 1600's, are ghostly reminders of desperate clashes with corsairs.

A STRATEGIC BULWARK

The human imprint on the Dry Tortugas is most evident on Garden Key, where Fort Jefferson broods over the dancing turquoise waters. With walls 50 feet high and 8 feet thick, a perimeter of almost half a mile, and three weapon tiers designed for 450 cannons, the massive fort was intended to control traffic along the Gulf of Mexico shipping lanes.

Though construction began on Garden Key in 1846 and continued for 30 years, the fort was never completed. With the introduction of the rifled cannon, masonry forts became obsolete by 1866. While the fort's guns were never fired in battle, its walls served as a military prison for Union army deserters during the Civil War. Condemned for their part in Abraham Lincoln's assassination, four "Lincoln Conspirators" were incarcerated here in 1865.

Visitors can enter the cell of Dr. Samuel Mudd, the Maryland physician who unwittingly set assassin John Wilkes Booth's leg in the hours following the president's murder. Mudd was pardoned after tending to 270 men struck by a 1867 outbreak of yellow fever. Following a second epidemic and a hurricane, the fort was abandoned in 1874, but was used as a navy wireless station in the early 1900's and served for a few months as a seaplane base in World War I.

A moat, half a mile in length, still surrounds the haunting walls of the hexagonal fort. The stone archways of the cannon tiers guard the remains of the officers' quarters, soldiers' barracks, two magazines, and a cistern—a vital feature on the waterless island. Visitors can watch a spectacular sunset from the fort and spend the night at a 10-site primitive campground located on a grassy area just outside the ramparts.

FOR MORE INFORMATION:

Dry Tortugas National Park, c/o Everglades National Park, P.O. Box 279, Homestead, FL 33030; 305-242-7700

Once known as the Gibraltar of the Gulf, Fort Jefferson was the largest in the chain of coastal fortifications stretching from Maine to Texas.

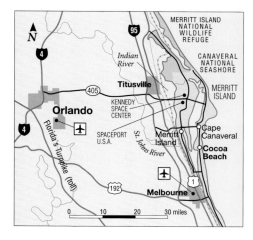

With its graceful long neck and characteristic yellow beak, the great egret is one of the largest wading birds to be seen on Merritt Island.

As a great blue heron casually lifts off from a salt marsh, the roar of massive rocket engines signals another successful space shuttle launch. This is Merritt Island, the home of Kennedy Space Center, Merritt Island National Wildlife Refuge, and Canaveral National Seashore, and one of the few places in the nation where progress and preservation share common ground.

The 70-acre portion of Merritt Island administered by NASA is surrounded by more than 156,000 acres of unspoiled land and water, where visitors can spot more endangered species than at any other national wildlife refuge. Located midway between Jacksonville and West Palm Beach, the island offers opportunities for fishing, boating, hunting, and wildlife watching, as well as exciting glimpses of space travel.

Along the national seashore's 24 miles of undeveloped sand dunes and barrier beach, anglers can hook scrappy bluefish, whiting, or pompano. Boardwalks allow visitors access to beaches without damaging the fragile vegetation of the sand dunes. The roots of sea oats, prickly pear, beach berry, and saw palmetto stabilize the 20-foot-high dunes and provide important nesting areas for indigo snakes and gopher tortoises. Giant loggerhead and green sea turtles nest on the beach.

The salt marshes are excellent sites for viewing roseate spoonbills, Louisiana herons, brown pelicans, snowy egrets, and peregrine falcons. The birds feast on a plentiful diet of snails, crabs, worms, clams, and fish. Black Point Wildlife Drive leads bird-watchers through Merritt Island's impounded marshes and pine flatwoods.

THE WAY TO THE STARS

At Spaceport USA—the visitor complex for Kennedy Space Center—five-story twin IMAX theaters show spectacular footage of space flight, while the Gallery of Spaceflight

Museum displays telephone booth–sized models of *Mercury*, *Gemini*, and *Apollo* space capsules. Stretching 60 feet longer than a football field, an authentic *Saturn* rocket dominates the Rocket Garden. At the other end of the garden is the Astronauts Memorial, an enormous granite monument

commemorating the 16 astronauts who lost their lives during NASA missions, nine of them during the 1986 *Challenger* disaster.

Official buses allow passengers to venture farther into the Space Center. The Blue Tour takes visitors to old launchpads at Cape Canaveral Air Force Station and to the Air Force Space Museum, where they can learn about the history of rocketry amid displays of spacecraft and winged missiles bearing such names as Matador, Navaho, Mace, and Hound Dog.

The Red Tour stops near active launchpads A and B, NASA Headquarters, and the Vehicle Assembly Building—an eight-acre complex that is one of the world's largest structures. No sight is more awe-inspiring than a shuttle liftoff. By reservation, visitors may view launches from within the center just six miles away from the launch area: a flash of light signals another journey out of the unique world of Merritt Island.

FOR MORE INFORMATION:

Titusville Area Chamber of Commerce, 2000 South Washington Ave., Titusville, FL 32780; 407-267-3036.

Rocket Garden displays many of the rockets and satellites used in the U.S. space program.

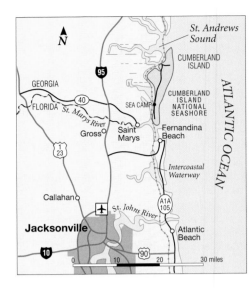

Live oaks thrive in the maritime forest that covers approximately 40 percent of the island's interior. The sharp-bladed leaves of saw palmettos are in the foreground.

The traces of human habitation have always been faint on Georgia's largest and southernmost barrier island, and nature prefers it that way. Except for the tracks left by shorebirds, footprints are rare along the 18 miles of Cumberland's shoreline. This narrow 40-square-mile sea island slumbers in isolation off the Atlantic coast despite the fact that Congress named it a national seashore in 1972. The National Park Service restricts access in order to protect the isle's fragile marine wilderness: a maximum of 300 visitors are allowed each day, and permits must be obtained for overnight camping.

A ferry service from St. Marys brings passengers past the marshes of Cumberland Sound, where seaside sparrows, marsh wrens, and pelicans find shelter in the grasslands. Here in the rich tidal streams interlaced on the island's western shore, ocean and river sediments nourish oysters, clams, fiddler crabs, conches, shrimp, and flounder. The Timucuan Indians inhabited the island for more than 3,000 years, subsisting on a diet of oysters, whose discarded shells were later used to build plantation homes. Cedar trees thrive in the alkaline soil left behind when millions of the oyster shells eroded.

SEASIDE BOARDWALK

When passengers disembark at either Dungeness or Sea Camp, they can explore the island by means of walking trails. The Dungeness, the River, and the Nightingale trails link up for a perfect day hike. A boardwalk follows the white seashore at Sea Camp Beach. Visitors who bathe in the surf should keep a sharp eye out for shorebirds and loggerhead turtles. The turtles, seen mainly at night on the beach, breed among the sand dunes.

The ruined Dungeness Mansion, built in 1884, is one of the attractions along the Dungeness Trail.

More than half the area of Cumberland Island—about 15,000 acres—consists of a dense maritime forest of cabbage palm, magnolia, American holly, devilwood, and pine. A tolerance to salt spray allows live oaks to dominate along the forest edge, but farther inland muscadine vines grow as thick as a human leg. Here, too, can be found thorny devil's walking sticks and resurrection ferns—aptly named because their fronds turn brown and shrivel up during periods of drought, only to flourish green again after a rainstorm.

People have inhabited Cumberland Island for thousands of years but have left behind few traces of their settlements. Revolutionary War general Nathanael Greene purchased land on the island in 1783. His widow built a four-story tabby home made of crushed oyster shells, which she named Dungeness. A century later Thomas Carnegie, the younger brother of financier Andrew, built a lavish 40-room summer home on the ruins of the original Greene house. Only a skeleton remains of the home, which was destroyed by a fire in 1959, but the stables, carriage houses, and servants' quarters bear witness to the island's opulent past. The ice house is now a museum dedicated to the early native inhabitants of the island.

Today pockets of Cumberland Island remain in private hands, including the sandspit at the northernmost tip—an area called Little Cumberland. The Carnegie heirs have converted a 1,300-acre family retreat into the exclusive Grayfield Inn. Another residence, the Plum Orchard Mansion, is not open to public tours.

Hardy hikers can head for Cumberland's humbler abodes at the Sea Camp campground, where sites are carved out of the dense palmetto undergrowth. They can listen to the sounds of horses' hooves in the distance, and perhaps catch a glimpse of the wild horses that roam the dunes. Like so many island tales of failed settlement, the horses are said to be all that remain of Spanish attempts to colonize the island.

FOR MORE INFORMATION:
Cumberland Island National Seashore, P.O. Box 806, St. Marys, GA 31558; 912-882-4335.

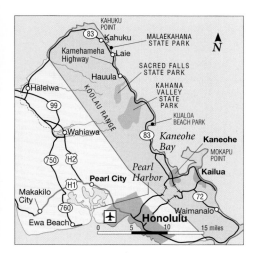

Diamond-shaped Oahu's northeast coast is the ideal location for exploring Hawaii's natural treasures and its cultural heritage. Also known as the Windward Coast, this is an area of sparkling turquoise waters, sheltered coves, misty volcanic ridges, and moist tropical forests—all within a day's drive from Honolulu. Scooped out of the steep Koolau Range, the rich valleys are blanketed with pastoral lands and dotted with tiny hamlets. Sweeping bays with broad palm-fringed shores meet windswept headlands.

In the southern arc of Kaneohe Bay, Kealohi Point offers a magnificent vista of Coconut Island, the desert isle featured on the television series *Gilligan's Island*. Travelers can view Kaneohe Bay's awe-inspiring coral reefs aboard glass-bottom boats, which leave from Heeia Kea Pier.

Kamehameha Highway weaves through rural valleys quilted with taro and sweet potato patches. At the wooden Waiahole Taro Factory, built in 1904, visitors can sample the starchy root vegetable. Backed by imposing Kanehoalani Ridge, the road passes Molii Fishpond, where mullet, moi, and tilapia thrive in the island's only continuously operating ancient fish hatchery.

Fiery wiliwili trees line the entry road to Kualoa Beach Park, a sacred place where chieftains once initiated their heirs into the art of leadership. At low tide visitors can wade out to Chinaman's Hat, a peaked island whose Hawaiian name, Mokolii, means "little lizard." Legend has it that the island is really the tail of a lizard slain by the goddess Hiiaka.

The Koolau Range has deep valleys notched into the steep volcanic mountains.

Makapuu Beach, near Makapuu Point, is one of the best places on the island for bodysurfing. A chunk of lava can be seen just offshore.

The wet climate of Kahana Valley State Park supports a lush forest of bamboo, mountain apple, guava, and ti—a plant traditionally used for thatching houses. In the upper valley, songs of native birds such as the apapane and amakihi mingle with the melodies of introduced species, including mynahs, cardinals, linnets, ricebirds, and doves. Lowland areas are covered with shrubs, hibiscus bushes, and hala—a small tree whose pineapplelike fruit was used by native Hawaiians as brushes for painting decorative barkcloth.

OFFERINGS TO THE GODS

The Nakoa Trail offers hikers the opportunity to pick seasonal tropical fruit and bathe in cool mountain streams. In nearby Sacred Falls State Park, Hawaiians still maintain the tradition of wrapping a ti leaf around rocks as an offering for the pig-god Kamapuaa. They have reason to try to appease the god: flash floods and falling rocks in the narrow gorge have claimed many lives. A muddy trail lined with apple trees leads to a popular swimming hole at the base of the waterfall before the trail reaches Kaliuwaa Falls' 80-foot drop.

Just northwest of Sacred Falls, Maakua Gulch towers 100 feet high and narrows in places to only a dozen feet across. Hikers can climb ridge trails on either side of the valley, or trek upstream to a restful pool behind Maakua Gulch.

At Malaekahana State Park, idyllic sandy shores are bordered by coconut palms, ironwood, and hala trees. Located just offshore, Moku Auia (Goat Island) is a seabird sanctuary with a white sandy cove that is perfect for swimming and snorkeling.

Passing old sugarcane fields and roadside stands selling shrimp and homegrown fruit, the road leads to Kahuku Point, the end of the eastern shore. During the winter immense waves—often reaching 20 feet to 30 feet in height—batter the Windward Coast, which continues to captivate visitors with its natural splendors.

FOR MORE INFORMATION:

Hawaii Visitors Bureau, 2270 Kalakaua Ave., Suite 801, Honolulu, HI 96815; 808-923-1811.

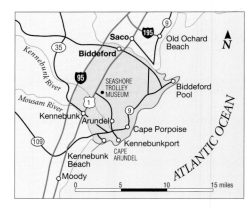

Cape Arundel provides a panoramic view of the sandy crescent of Kennebunk Beach, as well as the town of Kennebunkport. The beach is rarely crowded and seems to stretch for miles.

Travelers seeking a summer vacation by the sea with old-fashioned charm will find it in the small resort town of Kennebunkport. This picturesque fishing village lies on Maine's south coast, tucked between Cape Porpoise Harbor and the Kennebunk River.

Once a thriving shipbuilding center, Kennebunkport has long been a favorite getaway place for summer visitors. At the turn of the century, the town routinely offered a lively social calendar of dances, fairs, regattas, and social teas for well-heeled summer visitors. Writers and artists, including Booth Tarkington, flocked to this charming seaside community. In the 1920's historical novelist Kenneth Roberts popularized the area to the point that the town of North Kennebunk returned to its original name of Arundel—the title of one of his books—in the 1950's. Built in 1889, the Kennebunk River Club still stands on the banks of the Kennebunk River as a reminder of the town's heyday.

Today Kennebunkport is better known as the summer home of former president George Bush. In 1902 Bush's grandfather, George Walker, purchased an 11-acre peninsula that juts out into the sea at Cape Arundel. Walker built two palatial summer homes on the land, much to the consternation of locals, with whom the peninsula's coves, meandering woodland paths, juniper-scented sea breezes, and abundant sun-ripened blueberries had been popular for summer picnics.

ARCHITECTURAL CHARM

A short walk through the elm-shaded streets of Kennebunkport's historic district, along North and Maine streets and Ocean Avenue, reveals an architectural potpourri of stately homes. Built by sea captains and shipbuilders, the 18th- and 19th-century houses range in style from Colonial to Gothic and from Italianate to Second Empire, reflecting the changing tastes of the times. Some, such as the Captain Lord Mansion, have been converted into bed-and-breakfasts or inns. Built in the early 1800's by wealthy shipbuilder Capt. Nathanial Lord, Captain Lord Mansion is a three-and-a-half-story Federal-style home featuring a widow's walk and crowned with an octagonal cupola. The immaculately preserved Nott House was built in 1853 by merchant Charles Edwin Perkins and is open to the public. This Greek Revival mansion boasts a Doric colonnade and retains its original furnishings, carpets, and wallpaper. The diaries of Celia Perkins, the wife of Charles, provide visitors with a greater understanding of the early history of Kennebunkport.

Dock Square, Kennebunkport's commercial district, entices visitors with its array of specialty stores, which advertise their wares with hand-carved or hand-painted signs. In the summer months and on fall weekends, the riverside square is a mecca for serious buyers and casual window-shoppers alike.

After the hustle and bustle of Dock Square, the visitor may wish to slip across the Kennebunk River for a quiet walk along the silvery strand of Kennebunk Beach. Maine's south coast has the best beaches in the state, and the one here is particularly notable. At low tide, seabirds feed at the mouth of the Kennebunk River, and lobster boats bob gently on the horizon.

Kennebunkport is also the site of the world's largest collection of trolleys, housed just outside of town at the Seashore Trolley Museum. Established in 1939 by a group of trolley enthusiasts, the museum features a 1910 cable car from San Francisco, a rare 1941 double-decker trolley from Glasgow, Scotland, and a 1906 trolley car long since retired from New Hampshire's Manchester and Nashua Street Railway. Many of the museum's vehicles are maintained in working condition and take visitors on a four-mile round-trip along an old railroad right-of-way through the woods.

FOR MORE INFORMATION:
Kennebunk/Kennebunkport Chamber of Commerce, P.O. Box 740, Kennebunk, ME 04043; 207-967-0858.

Stacks of lobster traps attest to the fact that Kennebunkport is still an active fishing community, as well as a popular vacation destination.

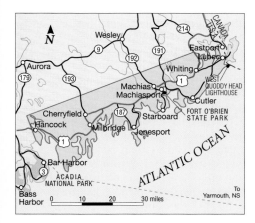

Shredded by ice-age glaciers, Maine's ragged eastern coast is edged with sharp peninsulas and fjordlike inlets. Historic fishing villages, blueberry fields, and nature preserves nestle in bays and valleys. While touring Maine's eastern coast from Eastport to Hancock, visitors encounter hospitable locals, pockets of Revolutionary history, and a scattering of tiny islands.

Eastport is the easternmost city on Maine's coastal fringe. An international shipping center, the port's livelihood depends on the fishing and salmon aquaculture industries. Located on Moose Island, Eastport's historic waterfront features the restored homes of local sea captains, oceanside art exhibitions, and theater productions. Red tugboats decorate the bay; charter boats offer deep-sea fishing and whale-watching excursions. Visitors can ogle Old Sow—the world's second-largest natural whirlpool—from a car ferry headed for Deer Island, in the Canadian province of New Brunswick. The swirling eddy is caused by extreme variations of high and low tides.

Early risers who visit West Quoddy Head Lighthouse, located near Lubec, are the first in the nation to see the sun rise. A 483-acre park located next to the candy-striped sentinel offers trails that lead to raised coastal peat bogs, providing spectacular views of the coastline.

Machias Seal Island affords bird enthusiasts the opportunity to spot Atlantic puffins. Machias itself was one of New England's first settlements. Once a leader in the lumber industry, the town's historic sites predate the Revolutionary War. Listed on the National Register of Historic Places, Burnham Tavern, erected in 1770, was the meeting place of the men who fought the Revolution's first naval battle in June 1775. A cannon and the well-preserved earthworks at Fort O'Brien State Park overlook Machias Bay, where the battle took place. In nearby Machiasport, the area's seafaring history is recounted at Gates House, an early-1800's Federal-style home. A road from Machiasport leads to Bucks Harbor, where visitors can stroll along a multicolored pebble shore of jasper and volcanic rhyolite at Jasper Beach.

LOBSTER RACES

From Machias to Hancock County, the sea is dotted with picturesque islands, and the roadside fields are carpeted with white blueberry blossoms in the spring. At Roque Bluffs, bathers can dip into either a freshwater pond or the briny Atlantic Ocean. Lucky visitors may even glimpse migrating whales from the seaside park's sandy beach. Jonesport, host of the World's Fastest Lobster Boat Races every July 4, is located just across from Beals Island. Next to Beals Island, a 1,540-acre preserve on Great Wass Island provides a safe haven for seals, bald eagles, and razorbills.

Hancock County's Mount Desert Island is located within Acadia National Park. More than 50 miles of gravel paths lead hikers, bicyclists, and horseback riders through scenery that takes in lakes, beaches, and mountains. From the summit of Cadillac Mountain, visitors are rewarded with a 360-degree vista of the Atlantic Ocean, distant mountains, and the interior of the state. Visitors can learn about marine life at a waterfront oceanarium in Southwest Harbor, or take a ferry to the charming Cranberry Islands from Southwest or Northeast harbors; Bass Harbor ferries make regular trips to Swans Island.

Back on the mainland, Ellsworth's elegant historic buildings mingle with modern structures. The steeple of the Greek Revival–style First Congregational Church is a Maine landmark, while stately Woodlawn, an 1820's Georgian mansion, commands a view across the Union River. A walking tour of the downtown district provides a glimpse of some of the town's other restored buildings.

The town of Blue Hill was named for the 940-foot promontory that offers views of Blue Hill Harbor, Penobscot Bay, and Acadia National Park. Visitors can stroll through this charming village and attend a chamber music concert at Kneisel Hall. Attracted by the area's primitive beauty, many artists and musicians make their summer home here.

FOR MORE INFORMATION:
Maine Office of Tourism, 189 State St., Station 59, Augusta, ME 04333; 207-287-5711.

Fishing boats at Bass Harbor on Mount Desert Island are a reminder of eastern Maine's continuing link with the sea.

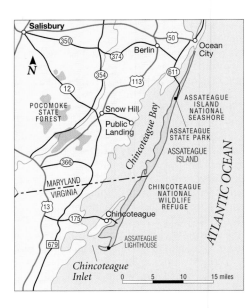

P recariously perched on the mid-Atlantic continental shelf, the fragile strip of barrier beach is the remnant of glacial debris washed down from the Appalachian Mountains thousands of years ago. Assateague was once linked to the mainland, and only became an island when the Great Hurricane of 1933, as it is known locally, carved an inlet just south of Ocean City. In 1955 the National Park Service considered Assateague too developed to fit the bill as a national seashore. Then in 1962 another strong storm leveled most of the existing private structures on the island, leaving the path clear for preservation.

Presently 37 miles long, the entire island is now a designated national seashore that straddles two states—the northern two-thirds of the island are in Maryland and the remainder in Virginia. The island also contains both Assateague State Park in Maryland and the Chincoteague National Wildlife Refuge. The National Park Service maintains its headquarters on the mainland, at the northern end of Assateague. Chincoteague Island lies tucked inside a small hook of land at the southern end. Both ends of the island feature nature trails and easy access to beaches for exploring, surf casting, and beachcombing.

Strewn across the black-and-brown-streaked beaches is a kaleidoscope of pebbles, seaweed, shells, glass, driftwood, and shellfish. Speckled birds' eggs nestle in protected saucers of warm sand, and sandpipers scurry in elegant formation along the water's edge. Occasionally a harbor seal ventures this far south and comes ashore to inspect the pristine coast. Assateague's location on the Atlantic Flyway makes it a temporary home for seabirds and migratory butterflies; bird-watchers can spot piping

plovers, herons, peregrine falcons, snowy egrets, and other wildfowl enjoying the quiet marshes and ponds that lie behind the primary dunes.

TREASURE SEEKERS

English colonel Henry Norwood was abandoned by his shipmates on Assateague on January 3, 1650, as he sought fresh water en route to the Virginia colonies. His account of his subsequent trek on foot describes the graciousness of local Indians, about whom little is now known, although their language left the barrier islands with their lyrical names. (Chincoteague, for example, means "beautiful land across the waters.") Some claim that the infamous pirate Edward Teach, better known as Blackbeard, kept one of his 14 wives and other treasures on the island. Certainly the island's sheltered inlets allowed 18th-century pirates stealthy access to the mainland and to coastal shipping. Over the years fortune hunters have scoured Assateague for buried pirate booty.

Worn smooth by the relentless action of the Atlantic, the coastal side of Assateague is quite different from the salt marshes, tidal pockets, and islets that stretch along Chincoteague Bay. Like most barrier islands, Assateague is tenuously anchored in place by beach grasses and other species of plants, subject to the vagaries of weather and waves. Over time the sands shift to reveal glimpses of former features, such as bare stumps where once grew cedar trees; a candy-striped lighthouse is now much far-

Wild ponies are permitted to graze freely within Chincoteague National Wildlife Refuge.

ther inland from its original position, and the crumbled remains of fish factories are now smothered by sand.

The constant movement of wind and wave sometimes exposes a long-buried shipwreck. Local legend has it that the island's most famous residents—the wild Chincoteague ponies—perhaps arrived on the island as a result of the wreck of a Spanish galleon. Others believe that the ponies are descended from domestic horses put out to graze on the island in the 17th century. Although their origins are a mystery, the famous ponies of Assateague Island have been celebrated in song and book alike, beloved particularly by generations of children who pored over the "Misty" books by Marguerite Henry.

After years of life on Assateague, the ponies have reverted to a feral state. In recent years their numbers have been kept to several hundred, split between two small herds—one in each state. Their small, rotund stature is due to their diet of coarse grasses and seaweed and the quantities of salt they consume by drinking seawater. Each July the Virginia herd is rounded up and made to swim across the channel to Chincoteague Island for an auction—an event that attracts thousands of spectators. At other times, the ponies are best viewed from the observation platform on the Woodland Trail at the Virginia end of the island, and almost anywhere on the Maryland portion. Fortunate visitors are treated to the rare sight of Assateague's wild ponies galloping at daybreak through the foam at water's edge.

Although the ponies are Assateague's most popular inhabitant, the island is also home to 44 species of mammals, some of which are found in the offshore waters. The opossum, which is the only marsupial in North America, lives in the forested areas; the endangered Delmarva fox squirrel is protected within the Chincoteague National Wildlife Refuge; and bottlenose dolphins are often spotted in the surf along the island's beaches during the summer months. River otters fish in the bay, enjoying a diet of fish and crabs.

This beautiful strand of seashore offers visitors many opportunities for enjoyment, from strolling along the beach to fishing and digging for clams.

FOR MORE INFORMATION:
Assateague Island National Seashore, 7206 National Seashore Lane, Berlin, MD 21811; 410-641-1441.

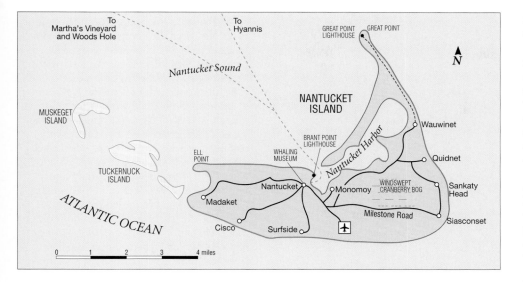

A profusion of brightly colored flowers adorns the weathered exterior of a fisherman's cottage.

An "elbow of sand" is how Herman Melville described Nantucket Island in his seafaring classic, *Moby Dick*. Others have seen in its 14-mile-long silhouette the shape of a whale thrashing its tail upward in the blue Atlantic waters. Like its sister isle, Martha's Vineyard, Nantucket is marked by the sea. Its long sandy beaches, unspoiled dunes, and tranquil fishing spots lie off the coast of Massachusetts, 11 miles south of Cape Cod.

Ferries leave from Hyannis for the town of Nantucket, a resort legendary for its whaling history. After the first sperm whale was harpooned offshore in 1712, most of the town's Puritan settlers abandoned their small farms for the hope of prospering at sea. The leviathan's oil was much in demand as a fuel for lamps because its flame burned brightly without fumes. By the late 1770's, Nantucket Town was the whaling capital of North America.

The nautical glory days are recalled at the Whaling Museum on Broad Street, where relics include an oil press, the 43-foot-long skeleton of a finback whale, and fine examples of scrimshaw (sperm whale teeth) that locals carved into combs, corset stays, pie-crimpers, and other useful objects.

Georgian, Federal, and Greek Revival mansions built by wealthy whaling families line cobblestoned Main Street. Many of the houses, like the Three Bricks—a trio of identical houses built in the 1830's for merchant Joseph Starbuck's sons—sport whale ivory mortgage buttons on the newel posts, a local status symbol erected when debts were paid off. Every building has its tale, particularly the Pacific Club built by Capt. William Roth in 1771, two years before his ships *Dartmouth* and *Beaver* emptied their cargo of tea into Boston Harbor during the historic Boston Tea Party.

HISTORIC LANDMARKS

A visitor's pass grants access to the 13 town sites restored by the Nantucket Historic Association. These landmarks include the white-pillared Hawden House, with its silver doorknobs; the Thomas Macy Warehouse, where ships were outfitted for long voyages; and the plain gray clapboard house built by Nathaniel Macy in 1723. On Sunset Hill sits the island's oldest Quaker dwelling, the modest gray-shingled Jethro Coffin farmhouse, which was built in 1686 and is now a national historic landmark.

After the discovery of kerosene in 1858, Nantucket was saved from economic ruin by its growing popularity with vacationers. Today visitors are lured by the tranquillity of a town with neither neon signs nor traffic lights. At Congdon's Pharmacy, established in the 19th century, patrons can sit at an old-fashioned soda fountain.

Of Nantucket's 80 miles of beach, the most rugged are on the south shore near Cisco and Surfside. In comparison, the north shore waters are more placid. Offshore are the famed Nantucket shoals, where codfish, striped bass, bonito, bluefish, and mackerel still thrive. In winter Nantucket's prized bay scallops are dragged from the nearby Head of the Harbor.

To the north, past Quidnet and Wauwinet, stands the 70-foot-high Great Point Lighthouse, accessible only by foot. The tip of this barrier beach is a wildlife refuge for nesting terns and other birds. Anglers crowd Great Point in spring and fall, when the bluefish are biting.

At the heart of the the island lies the Windswept Cranberry Bog, more than 200 acres of preserved marshland, meadows, and ponds. In this tranquil spot, northern harriers and black-backed gulls soar freely above fields of bright red cranberry bushes.

FOR MORE INFORMATION:

Nantucket Visitor Services, 25 Federal St., Nantucket, MA 02554; 508-228-0925.

Located at the entrance to Nantucket Harbor, Brant Point Lighthouse alerts passing ships to potential perils.

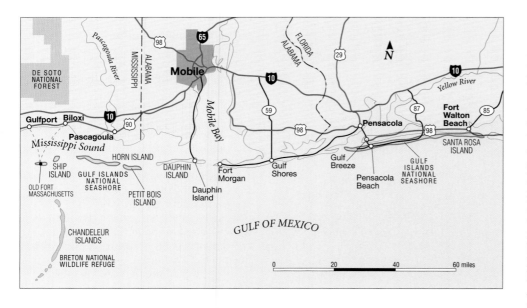

This rich patchwork of beach, bay, and bayou studded with wild barrier islands lies on the northern edge of the Gulf of Mexico, and stretches from Choctawhatchee Bay in the Florida Panhandle to Mississippi's West Ship Island. Largest of the 10 national seashores, the Gulf Islands National Seashore is an unforgettable experience for those who have curled their toes in the bone-white sandy beaches or explored the tranquillity of the bayous. As shoreline currents nibble away at their eastern ends and spit up sand to the west, the barrier islands are moving inexorably westward.

The Gulf Islands bear the brunt of violent winds and storms that would otherwise damage the fragile life of coastal marshes. Nurtured by the quiet blue-green waters between island and mainland, sea trout, southern flounder, and shrimp abound. On the Gulf side, dunes slope down to beaches of fine sand that are held in place by golden tassel-headed sea oats. The complex root system of this grass extends as much as 20 feet below the surface. Just beyond the dunes, twisted slash pine and scrub live oak attest to the stunting effect of salt spray. Here and there are inland thickets of beach elder and wax myrtle; the latter, like its close relation, the bayberry, produces a wax that can be used to make candles. Farther back, fresh water collects in marshes among old sand dunes, creating an ideal environment for alligators, raccoons, and—on Horn Island—bald eagles, which were reintroduced in 1986-89.

The Mississippi islands are accessible only by charter or private boats. Such isolation encourages visitors to slow down and marvel at the unhurried flight of a great blue heron or to feel the saw-toothed edge of a palmetto leaf stem.

ISLAND FORTRESS

Reaching West Ship Island is easier, since concession boat trips are offered from Gulfport in season. Originally West Ship Island and East Ship Island were one. In 1969, however, Hurricane Camille sent 200-mile-an-hour winds hurtling across the Gulf of Mexico, and a 30-foot tidal wave cut the island in two. A day at the beach here should include a tour of the cool interior of Fort Massachusetts. The fort still stands as a testimony to the ingenuity and persistence of the U.S. Army Corps of Engineers.

Across the Mississippi Sound and into Davis Bayou, a farther section of the national seashore caps Stark Bayou. Self-

More than 21.5 million bricks were used to build Fort Pickens, constructed by the U.S. Army from 1829 to 1834.

guided tours in the coastal forest sometimes reveal an armadillo rooting for ants and termites in decaying logs. Stepping softly through the loblolly pines, a walker may hear the guttural burp of bullfrogs.

At Johnson Beach on Perdido Key, one of the areas protected by the Florida district of Gulf Islands, a little sleuthing along the water's edge invariably turns up brightly colored coquinas and intricate whelk shells amid the scurrying of mole crabs. At the Naval Live Oaks Area on the mainland, middens (rubbish piles) and other remains help archeologists to understand and chronicle the long period of Indian settlement. On Santa Rosa Island, the shadowy bastions of Fort Pickens—built by slave labor in the 1830's—conceal the spacious living quarters of Geronimo, the great Apache chief, and his small band of warriors, who were imprisoned here for two years beginning in 1886.

FOR MORE INFORMATION:

Mississippi District: Superintendent, Gulf Islands National Seashore, 3500 Park Rd., Ocean Springs, MS 39564; 601-875-9057. Florida District: Superintendent, Gulf Islands National Seashore, 1801 Gulf Breeze Pkwy., Gulf Breeze, FL 32561; 904-934-2600.

A great blue heron takes a solitary stroll along the Gulf Islands National Seashore.

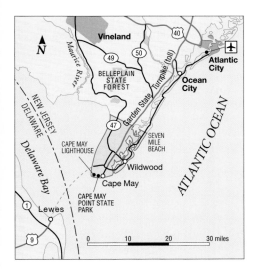

Cape May's temperate climate was first remarked upon by the Dutch navigator Cornelius Jacobsen Mey as he explored Delaware Bay back in the 1620's: he liked it so much he named the cape after himself. Whaling colonies were established on the peninsula, first by the Dutch and later by New England whaler-yeomen in pursuit of migratory whales down the mid-Atlantic coast. Over time, Cape May's favorable position at the confluence of the Atlantic Ocean and Delaware Bay led it to become a center for coastal trade, and its glorious summer weather guaranteed its reputation as a genteel spot in which to retire when the weather elsewhere became uncomfortable.

As early as the 1760's, sojourners—as the early tourists were called—fled the sweltering heat of urban summers to recuperate in this quiet seaside town. Cape May's heyday was in the 19th century, when steamships and then the railroad brought summer visitors in droves. Drawn by the cool summer breezes that sweep over the peninsula and the town's languorous pace, well-heeled visitors returned year after year to take long carriage rides along the hard-packed sand beaches, swim in the ocean, and attend concerts conducted by John Philip Sousa. Evenings were spent dancing and dining in grand settings such as the Mt. Vernon Hotel, designed to sleep 3,000 guests and seat 2,000 in its dining room.

In 1878 a great fire destroyed 30 blocks of hotels and summer homes. Fortunately the proprietors who summered here were wealthy enough to rebuild, and some of their "cottages" still grace the town. With competition from Atlantic City during the 1900's, however, Cape May suffered a long period of decline.

A second disaster altered the course of Cape May's history when, in the 1960's, a devastating storm ripped through the resort, reducing the boardwalk, beach, and many of the beachfront buildings to shambles. Residents were faced with a difficult choice: demolish the splendid remnants of a bygone era and replace them with the glass-and-metal high-rises so popular in other New Jersey seaside resorts, or rebuild with a view toward preserving the town's unique Victorian character and charm.

A TREASURE PRESERVED

Contemporary visitors to Cape May can easily see the outcome of this struggle: the city's tranquil streets are lined with so many 19th-century structures that Cape May has been designated a National Historic Landmark. A stroll through town is a walk back through time—every inn, guest house, and private home still reflects the town's original Victorian flavor. Towers, cupolas, and turrets decorate these quaint dwellings. For those with a taste for the finer details, there are plenty of barge-boards, pendants, spandrels, and finials to reinforce the feel of a bygone era. Visitors can take a carriage tour of the stately mansions, where shady verandas conjure up inviting images of ice-cold lemonade, creaky porch swings, and somnolent cats.

During the summer, the beach below the rebuilt promenade is strewn with brightly colored umbrellas. Today's casually dressed summer visitor is a distant cry from the Victorian ladies who would emerge at 11:00 A.M. sharp, decorously attired in head-to-toe bathing gear to go swimming.

Ambling along the Atlantic shore at Sunset Beach, beachcombers can root for the smooth quartz pebbles that are known as Cape May diamonds or take a look at a World War I ship, the U.S.S. *Atlantis*, partially sunk offshore. In the early mornings, zealous anglers take over the docks at Cape May Harbor, while braver souls sample deep-sea fishing aboard a charter boat. Coast Guard recruits receive their basic training at the Cape May Training Center, and visitors are welcome to attend the weekly graduation ceremonies.

In keeping with the tenor of the town, the yearly calendar is filled with events such as a spring tulip festival, a midsummer kite festival, and a week in the autumn when the town celebrates its Victorian heritage. During the month of December, local inns are decked out in Dickensian yuletide decoration that transforms the town.

Two miles from town, beside the little borough of Cape May Point, the Cape May Point State Park offers naturalist-guided tours of the marshes and dunes, where flying squirrels, red foxes, river otters, and muskrats find a protected home. Bird lovers soon discover why this area and the neighboring Cape May Migratory Bird Refuge enjoy a reputation as a birder's mecca. The region is located on the Atlantic Flyway, and on a good day visitors may see as many as 150 species of migrating birds. During the summer glossy ibis, snowy egrets, and spiraling hawks are commonly sighted in the bright blue sky.

FOR MORE INFORMATION:
Cape May Chamber of Commerce, P.O. Box 556, Cape May, NJ 08204; 609-884-5508.

A colorful array of Victorian buildings, many of them adorned with verandas, overlooks the ocean.

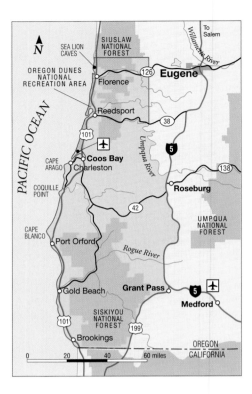

About halfway down the Pacific Coast of Oregon, rugged headlands give way to miles of sand dunes that undulate and sparkle in the sunlight. The dunes preview Oregon's striking southern coast, where vast beaches, waterfront towns, and seaside overlooks are loosely strung together by Coast Highway 101. Along this craggy coastline, waves crash against basalt cliffs, while fat Steller's sea lions bask on offshore rocks, and barnacle-covered whales cruise the frigid waters.

Just north of Florence, visitors can get a close-up look at a sea lion rookery at Sea Lion Caves. The mammals congregate here during fall and winter, raising their young on ledges during the warmer months. An elevator leads 208 feet down to a streaked cavern, which stretches the length of a football field. Aboveground, the site affords a picture-perfect view of Heceta Head Lighthouse, a coastal sentinel since 1894.

Poised at the mouth of Siuslaw River, Florence retains vestiges of its 19th-century fishing village origins, while the delicately arched Siuslaw River Bridge is a fine example of the 1930's Art Deco style. Visitors can fish the Siuslaw River for salmon, trout, and steelhead, or frolic in the ocean surf.

From Siuslaw River giant sand dunes replace volcanic cliffs for 47 miles. Covering 31,500 acres, Oregon Dunes National

The brilliant yellow flowers of Scotch broom brighten the seashore at Coquille Point.

Recreation Area's dunes reach heights of 500 feet. A 12,440-acre section of the area is open to dirt bikes and dune buggies, as well as four-wheel-drive vehicles. The rest of the park is covered in tranquil rolling sand hills and woods, inhabited by black bears, black-tailed deer, and tundra swans. Nature walks along 30 miles of trails offer visitors a chance to see salmonberries, huckleberries, Pacific rhododendrons, and seashore lupines, which thrive in the park.

TIMBER COUNTRY

The nation's largest expanse of coastal dunes comes to a halt just north of Coos Bay in North Bend. Coos Bay itself is a bustling harbor, exporting more timber than any other port in the world. Visitors can charter a boat to watch the migrations of gray whales, or take a tour of a myrtle-wood factory, where craftspeople fashion the hardwood into salt and pepper shakers, bowls, clocks, and furniture. The multihued wood is unique to a small area on the Pacific Coast; burls and unusual grain patterns add to its richness and distinct beauty.

Nearby Charleston boasts an area where craggy cliffs alternate with uncrowded beaches. Cape Arago is an excellent vantage point for viewing sea lions and pods of breaching gray whales. Whale watchers are most likely to spot these huge mammals in the morning hours, from December through the month of May.

Dank bogs between Coos Bay and the town of Bandon are covered with bright cranberries in the fall. Visitors can watch harvesters corral the floating berries to the side of the bog after rotary blades have clipped the fruit from the stalk. Along Bandon's waterfront, squabbling seagulls circle above basalt sea stacks. Low wooden buildings evoke the frontier days in Old Town, where quaint shops showcase the wares of local potters and sculptors.

Siskiyou National Forest begins near Port Orford and stretches to California. Delicate ferns unfurl beneath canopies of Douglas firs and bigleaf maples. In the Loeb Park section of the forest, hikers can ramble through a riverside myrtle grove and gaze in awe at 300-foot-high redwoods.

Winding through an old-growth forest near Humbug Mountain, a three-mile-long trail is scented with wild bay leaves and decorated with tiger lilies, Indian pipes, and bleeding hearts. Broad views of the Pacific Ocean from the top of Humbug Mountain are well worth the 1,756-foot climb.

Mountain bikers can explore remnants of a 19th-century road along Lower Rogue River Trail near Gold Beach, where gold was found among grains of sand in the 1850's. Traveling through the Rogue's rapids in a jet boat, avid wildlife watchers may catch glimpses of bears, deer, eagles, and ospreys. The southern coast's natural beauty has weathered the transition to modern life very well.

FOR MORE INFORMATION:
Oregon Tourism Commission, 775 Summer St. N.E., Salem, OR 97310; 800-547-7842.

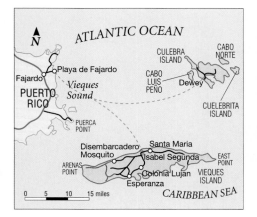

Built on Vieques Island in 1843, Fortín Conde de Mirasol was the first Spanish fort to be erected in the New World. The fort now serves as a museum.

Puerto Rico's best-kept vacation secret may just be the sister islands of Culebra and Vieques. Also known as the Spanish Virgin Islands, these two tiny tropical gems lie off the east coast of Puerto Rico midway between the city of San Juan and the island of St. Thomas in the U. S. Virgin Islands.

Columbus reportedly first sighted the islands during his second voyage in 1493. Culebra and Vieques were subsequently colonized by the Spanish, who decimated the native Taino Indian population. At the end of the Spanish-American War in 1898, Spain formally ceded Culebra and Vieques to the United States.

Culebra offers beautiful white-sand beaches and warm clear waters. More than 80 percent of its coastline is coral reef. Squirrel fish, parrot fish, sergeant majors, and groupers dart among young and old formations of brain, finger, elkhorn, and fire coral. The clear shallow waters make this underwater paradise easily accessible to even inexperienced snorkelers.

One quarter of Culebra, including 23 islands, rocks, and cays, is occupied by the Culebra National Wildlife Refuge. The island is a favorite nesting site of more than 85 species of birds, including terns, boobies, laughing gulls, Caribbean martins, ospreys, and endangered brown pelicans. Sooty terns are the most numerous and nest on Culebra between May and October.

Other Atlantic visitors include four species of sea turtle—the Atlantic loggerhead and green sea turtle, the hawksbill, and the endangered leatherback, which lays its eggs on the shoreline sands.

In the 1940's, President Roosevelt placed both Culebra and Vieques in the hands of the U.S. Navy. The navy built an ammunition depot on the west of Vieques, as well as a training facility on the east, and moved most of the population into the 13 square miles left between its outposts. The navy still controls more than two-thirds of

26,000-acre Vieques. Paradoxically, the military presence has helped to preserve Vieques' natural beauty and ecology, protecting the land from extensive development.

Vieques has a population of approximately 8,000 residents, most of whom live in or around Isabel Segunda. Spanish influence is still strongly evident in this sleepy, attractive town, with its pastel houses, bustling harbor, and lively plaza.

From Isabel Segunda, a four-mile drive through verdant, rolling hills dotted with cattle leads to Esperanza. Once a center for the sugarcane industry, which flourished on the island from the 1840's until the 1920's, Esperanza is now a quiet fishing village. Many of the former plantation homes have been converted into hotels.

BEACH PARADISE

The allure of Vieques is its sea, sand, and surf. The island has more than 40 golden sandy beaches, fringed with coconut palm and sea grape trees that descend gently into warm aquamarine waters. Beach lovers can take their pick, from Sombe or Sun Bay—a one-and-a-half-mile-long crescent just east of Esperanza—to the enclosed half-moon of Media Luna, or the seclusion of Navio and the prosaically named navy beaches: Red, Green, and Blue.

During the day, Vieques beaches offer sunlit serenity, but on moonless nights

The pastel stucco that adorns this house on Culebra Island is typical of the tropical style of architecture seen in the island's residences.

Mosquito Bay is the site of magic. When the sun sets, the bay's shallow waters display their treasures of microscopic plankton that give off a phosphorescent glow—an eerie incandescent blue-white glimmer—when disturbed. One of the world's few unspoiled bioluminescent bays, Mosquito Bay is just one of the islands' many riches.

FOR MORE INFORMATION:
Tourism Company of Puerto Rico, P.O. Box 4435, Old San Juan Station, San Juan, PR 00905; 809-721-2400.

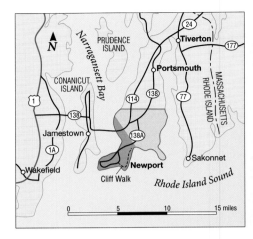

Extravagantly ornate wrought-iron gates lead to Belcourt Castle, built in 1892 by Richard Morris Hunt for Oliver Belmont. Belcourt Castle is just one of Newport's famed summer cottages.

When Rhode Islanders refer to "the glitter and the gold," rest assured that they speak of their largest, most-visited island, which sits snugly at the mouth of Narragansett Bay. During the Gilded Age, the rich came to Newport to build castles on the beach along the rugged cliffs of Rhode Island—an isle sometimes called Aquidneck by locals, to avoid confusion with the state name.

Highway 138 leads into the seaside town. Visitors arriving from Jamestown across the Newport Bridge are provided with a sweeping view of the harbor. Sun and surf are the prime attractions in Newport, but the summer resort is also legendary for the palatial summer "cottages" built in the1800's by some of New York's wealthiest families—among them the Vanderbilts, Astors, and Belmonts. This was a time of conspicuous consumption. There are tales of the Newport elite's baths with gold faucets, stables larger than the average American home, solid brass dining chairs, and even caviar for the dogs.

One of the best ways to catch a glimpse of these exclusive retreats is to take a stroll along Cliff Walk—a three-mile oceanside path that hugs the shore of Rhode Island Sound on one side, with the mansion grounds on the other. Another route, the famous Ocean Drive, loops around the peninsula, allowing motorists to view many prestigious addresses.

The Preservation Society of Newport County owns and operates six of the city's famed mansions—Kingscote, the Elms, Chateau-sur-Mer, Rosecliff, Marble House, and the fabulously ornate The Breakers, built by Cornelius Vanderbilt II in the style of a 17th-century Genoese palace. Marble House cost William K. Vanderbilt $11 million to build. Rosecliff was built by Stanford White in 1902 to resemble the Grand Trianon at Versailles—complete with a Court of Love inspired by that of French queen Marie Antoinette. During the Newport Music Festival, held annually in July, several of the mansions' ballrooms, including the opulent Great Hall at The Breakers, play host to world-class chamber music concerts.

WEALTH OF HISTORY

Newport's famous vacationers include John F. Kennedy, who wed Jacqueline Bouvier at nearby St. Mary's Church in 1953. Even at Trinity Church, which has dominated the skyline since 1726, visitors cannot escape the presence of Newport's wealthy patrons. As they kneel to pray, as did George Washington many years ago, the image of Cornelius Vanderbilt—clad as a knight in armor—gazes out from a Tiffany window.

For history buffs, the Historic Hill area offers wealth of a different kind: a collection of colonial buildings that rivals even those found in Colonial Williamsburg. More than 200 sites around the Point and Washington Square date from the 17th, 18th, and 19th centuries.

The town offers a charming 90-minute walking tour that takes in highlights such as the 1675 Wanton Lyman-Hazard House and the Hunter House, bedecked with fine colonial furniture. At the Old Colony House, now a national historic landmark, Newport's citizens heard the Declaration of Independence proclaimed from the second-floor balcony.

Along the walk, some of the buildings passed evoke Newport's beginnings as a seaport in the mid-1600's, when Quakers, Jews, Baptists, and other religious refugees arrived. Several sites are "firsts" for the nation: the 1699 Quaker Meeting House is now the oldest religious building in America; the Touro Synagogue, established in 1763, was the first Jewish house of worship; and the Redwood Library, which opened in 1750, was the nation's first library. Less cerebral is the White Horse Tavern: in operation since 1673, it is America's oldest surviving tavern.

Some of the country's finest topiary—shrubs and trees pruned in the shapes of animals or geometric designs—are found at Green Animals Topiary Gardens, in the town of Portsmouth. Visitors are advised not to overlook the other riches of Rhode Island—the trees, the sea air, the beaches, and the summer activities. Amid the pomp and glamour of the glittering social season, locals stage equally worthy events such as the annual public clambake and Newport's Great Chowder Cookoff.

FOR MORE INFORMATION:
Newport Convention and Visitors Bureau, 23 America's Cup Ave., Newport, RI 02840; 800-326-6030 or 401-849-8048.

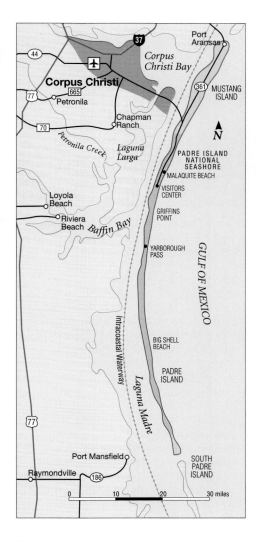

Sunset bathes the dune grass ridges on Padre Island, overlooking the Gulf of Mexico.

It was first christened Isla Blanca, meaning "white island," for the whiteness of its beaches by Spanish explorer Alonso de Pineda in 1519. Today it is called Padre Island, after Padre José Nicolas Balli, a missionary-turned-rancher who settled on the island in 1804.

The building of the Mansfield Channel in 1964 cut the land— once a single, long, thin wedge of sand, dune, and grassland—in two, dividing it into northern Padre Island and South Padre Island. Together they faithfully follow the eastern Gulf shore of Texas, protecting the mainland from the whiplash of tropical storms and hurricanes. Wind and rain sweep more sand away from Padre Island than is deposited by the Gulf of Mexico. As it shrinks, it slithers closer to the mainland. South Padre, on the other hand, appears to be growing in size.

PADRE'S REEF

The horizon off both islands offers a view of water and sky uncluttered by oil rigs— an increasingly rare sight along the Texan coast. Deep beneath the Gulf, however, the story is a different one: here a sunken steel forest of oil rigs and World War II Liberty ships form a long chain of artificial reefs. Intrepid scuba divers make expeditions 50 miles offshore, where the waters become crystal clear. Exploring the silent world of this artificial microcosm, divers can mingle freely with tropical fish such as French angels and glistening jacks, and come face-to-face with stingrays, angelfish, barracuda, and butterfly fish.

Closer to shore, the waters are rumored to hide cargoes of Aztec gold and silver from the hulls of Spanish galleons blown off course en route from Mexico to Spain. Occasionally gray, sand-scoured coins (now belonging to the state of Texas) turn up on the beaches, but sharp eyes are more likely to pick out treasures of a different sort: a lightning whelk, Texas' state shell; a spiky eastern murex; or a fighting conch—an animal that carries its home on its back. A fortunate few may even spot a Kemp's Ridley sea turtle or a nest of hatchlings. An adult turtle may have been transported from a Mexican beach when still an egg, incubated, and deposited on Padre Island. On South Padre Island, Ila Loetscher, known locally as the Turtle Lady, has been pivotal in raising public awareness in the struggle to save this endangered species.

Padre Island National Seashore has a small, first-come-first-served campground in the Malaquite Beach area. Farther south, 55 inviting miles of Gulf beach are open to four-wheel-drive vehicles. At Yarborough Pass, a primitive campsite overlooks the shallow waters of Laguna Madre.

In contrast, South Padre has become a magnet for visitors. With the building of the channel, the island was thrown into a frenzy of development of hotels, condominiums, shops, and restaurants. The constant southeasterly breezes and shallow waters of Laguna Madre make it a perfect site for windsurfing: in May each year the island hosts one of the continent's largest windsurfing tournaments.

Although South Padre is more developed than Padre Island, there are still times of the year and places along the shore where visitors can pass solitary days fishing or digging for coquina clams on beaches that were formed more than 4,500 years ago. Backing the beaches, undulating sand dunes are anchored by the roots of sea oats and the delicate interlacing of plants such as beach croton, evening primrose, and beach morning glory. Hidden under an unmarked sand dune called Money Hill lies a fortune in 19th-century coins and jewelry buried here by John Singer (the brother of the man who patented the Singer sewing machine) and Joanna Singer, whose pro-Union sentiments forced them to flee the island as the Civil War loomed. The shifting dunes transformed the landscape, and the Singers were never able to recover their treasure.

FOR MORE INFORMATION:

South Padre Island Convention and Visitors Bureau, P.O. Box 3500, South Padre Island, TX 78597; 800-343-2368.

Sharp-eyed visitors may spot the elusive lizards that inhabit the dunes of Padre Island.

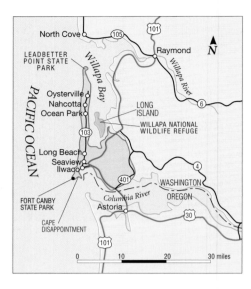

Some of the roughest water in the world is found where the Columbia River flows into the Pacific Ocean. Powerful currents and treacherous bars have earned this region the title of the "Graveyard of the Pacific." A busy Coast Guard station operates out of Cape Disappointment, which is also home to the only Motor Lifeboat School in the United States. Here students from marine services around the world learn how to handle boats in the turbulent seas often found at the mouths of rivers.

In a snug little cove below the lighthouse at Cape Disappointment lies Waikiki Beach. Swimming in the ocean here is strongly discouraged. At nearby North Head, visitors can often spot gray whales as they journey southward and northward to their wintering and summering grounds.

Two thousand acres of land stretching from Cape Disappointment to Beard's Hollow comprise Fort Canby State Park. Once an active military installation guarding the mouth of the Columbia River, the fort was named in 1875 for Gen. Edward Canby, who in 1865 received the surrender of the last Confederate armies. Old bunkers and batteries share the grounds with hiking trails that weave through dense forest, broken by views of Benson Beach.

LOCAL INDUSTRIES

On the eastern side, Long Beach Peninsula buffers Willapa Bay from the open sea, creating a pristine estuary ideal for oyster farming. The port at Nahcotta hums with the sounds of the gathering, opening, canning, processing, and shipping of oysters. A newly opened interpretive center weaves together more than 100 years of history about the oyster industry. Up and down the peninsula, the exteriors of shops, banks, and other businesses are decorated with

Bright red cranberries flourish in the bogs of Long Beach Peninsula. The berries are harvested in the autumn.

murals illustrating local history. Some of the paintings bring to life the major industries of the region; others faithfully depict scenes from the peninsula's pioneer days, such as a stagecoach driving along the beach at Seaview or a steamer pulling up at the docks in Ilwaco. The visitor center in Long Beach provides information on the 16 murals from Chinook to Ocean Park.

Leadbetter State Park, a wildlife refuge located beyond Ocean Park, is a stopover for some 100 species of migrating birds. The park marks the northern limit of the breeding range for the snowy plover, which nests in sand along the shore. Sandpipers, sanderlings, yellowlegs, and a sea goose known as the brant may be spotted along the park's many hiking trails.

Spring is the time for the jazz festival in the town of Long Beach and for Ilwaco's fishing derby. Summer provides perfect conditions for the International Kite Festival in Long Beach, as well as a garlic festival in Ocean Park, where garlic-flavored ice cream, pizza, and pretzels are just a few of the delights to be sampled. In autumn the Ilwaco Museum holds its cranberry festival. Visitors can participate in the harvesting of one of the peninsula's best-loved crops—just one of the many unique experiences that this region has to offer.

FOR MORE INFORMATION:
Long Beach Peninsula Visitors Bureau, P.O. Box 562, Long Beach, WA 98613; 800-451-2542.

In the southwestern corner of Washington State, the coast crooks a finger of land northward into the Pacific Ocean, enclosing Willapa Bay and beckoning visitors to explore a rugged landscape of cliffs, beaches, and forests. From the rocky headlands in the south to the bayous in the north, Long Beach Peninsula is home to small communities that continue to harvest nature's bounty from the sea. Lying approximately halfway between Portland, Oregon, and Seattle, Washington, the peninsula is about 2.5 miles wide and 28 miles from end to end.

For years travelers to this part of the country took a 45-minute ferry ride across the Columbia River from Astoria, Oregon. Now the Astoria-Megler Bridge brings travelers to the peninsula. On a clear day the trip affords a heart-stopping view of Mount St. Helens as it soars against the skyline, its white top slanted to one side as the result of the cataclysmic 1980 eruption.

Fort Canby State Park's Lewis and Clark interpretive center overlooks an almost vertical portion of the peninsula's coast.

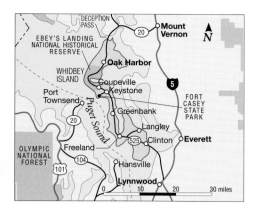

Admiralty Head Lighthouse, built in the early 20th century, now serves as Fort Casey's interpretive center. The center provides information about early coastal forts and the Puget Sound Defense System, which operated from 1900 to the beginning of World War II.

Two centuries ago, Capt. George Vancouver was told by his ship's master, Joseph Whidbey, that the waters known as Port Gardiner actually formed a narrow strait between two islands. So informed, he called the strait Deception Pass and gave Whidbey's name to one of the region's many islands. Although Whidbey is the largest island in the lower 49 states, no point on this serpentine crescent of land is more than five miles from the sea, due to its meandering coastline, which is deeply pocketed with bays and inlets.

Two hundred feet below Deception Pass Bridge, the sea becomes a churning maelstrom with the turning tide. Across the bridge lies Deception Pass State Park, one of Washington State's most-visited parks. Here great blue herons stalk amid beaver dams on marshy Cranberry Lake, and the island's highest point—Goose Rock—provides sea vistas that stretch north to Victoria, British Columbia, and west to the majestic snowcapped Olympic Mountains.

Whidbey's moderate climate averages 20 inches of rain a year. Severe weather is rare, but shipwrecks testify to the ocean's force and the difficulty of navigating the treacherous currents around the island's sheer cliffs and rocky beaches. Inland the landscape is composed of meadows and pine forests, interspersed with freshwater lakes and rolling tracts of farmland.

Bald eagles, deer, elks, and coyotes may be spotted from Highway 20, which connects the Naval Air Station with Oak Harbor, the island's largest community. Named for its abundance of Garry oaks, some now five centuries old, this quaint 19th-century sea captains' town was settled by Norwegian, Swiss, Yankee, Irish, and finally Dutch immigrants. Their legacy is a blue-and-white windmill at the Holland Gardens, repainted each spring for a festival that celebrates the city's heritage.

Just south of Oak Harbor the pristine waters of finger-shaped Penn Cove, once a gathering place for Skagit Indians, are now filled with floating mussel farms. Hundreds of brightly colored ropes are suspended in the water, each one an annual home for up to 50 pounds of mussels.

BOUNTY OF LAND AND SEA

Coupeville, the state's second-oldest town, was named by Capt. Thomas George Coupe in 1852. He was so struck by the harbor and its surroundings that he declared to his wife he had found the Garden of Eden. Coupe's redwood home, as well as Victorian houses, false-fronted shops, and other historic structures line the streets of present-day Coupeville. The Island County Historical Museum contains pioneer and maritime memorabilia. The town retains its historical flavor due, in part, to its inclusion in Ebey's Landing National Historical Reserve. The first of its kind in the nation, this 22-square-mile reserve is named for Col. Isaac Neff Ebey. Much of the reserve is privately owned, but visitors are welcome to visit its two state parks: Fort Casey and Fort Ebey.

Fort Ebey's gentle walking trails provide dramatic vistas that overlook the Strait of Juan de Fuca and the fertile Ebey's Prairie and Rhododendron State Park to the east. Wildlife observation points provide the patient watcher with sightings of whales, harbor seals, and sea otters. An interpretive center at Admiralty Head Lighthouse recreates defense systems of a bygone era.

The island is carpeted with berries, both wild and cultivated. Whidbey's Greenbank Berry Farm boasts a vineyard and a turn-of-the-century red barn, where visitors can sample loganberry produce such as jams, pies, ice cream, wines, and liqueur.

Springtime is the perfect season to visit the Meerkerk Rhododendron Gardens, located just south of the tiny village of Greenbank. This is the time of year when thousands of brilliantly colored native and hybrid rhododendrons and azaleas, Japanese cherries, maples, and magnolias burst into bloom; five miles of trails wind through its woodland preserve of cedar, hemlock, and Douglas fir.

The Old West–style main street of Langley has become home to antique shops and bookstores. Founded by an enterprising German teenager, Jacob Anthes, this rustic town is now the cultural center of the island. A busy car ferry runs from Clinton to Mukilteo—fitting transport for an island that still retains so much of its maritime flavor and heritage.

FOR MORE INFORMATION:
Greater Oak Harbor Chamber of Commerce, P.O. Box 883, Oak Harbor, WA 98277; 360-675-3535.

INDEX

PICTURE CREDITS

Cover photograph by Jeff Gnass

2 Tom Till
5 Tom Till

CAPE COD
8 Tom Till
10 *(upper left)* Robert Perron
10 *(lower right)* Jeffrey D. Smith/Woodfin
Camp & Associates
12 *(upper left)* Alan Briere
12 *(lower left)* Alan Briere
12, 13 Glenn Van Nimwegen
14 Stephen Wilkes
14, 15 Jeffrey D. Smith/Woodfin Camp
& Associates
15 Robert Perron
16 *(upper left)* David Weintraub
16 *(lower)* Stephen Wilkes
16, 17 Stephen Wilkes
17 Glenn Van Nimwegen
18 Alan Briere
19 *(both)* Alan Briere

THE OUTER BANKS
20, 21 Fred Hirschmann
22 David Muench
24 Al Harvey
24, 25 David Muench
25 Carr Clifton
26 *(both)* John Elk
27 Randy Taylor
28 *(upper)* Fred Hirschmann
28 *(lower)* David Muench
30 Carol Shanks/Transparencies
31 *(upper)* Carol Shanks/Transparencies
31 *(lower)* Alan Briere

BISCAYNE NATIONAL PARK
32 Julie Robinson
34 *(both)* Timothy O'Keefe
36 James A. Kern
36, 37 Bob Miller
37 James A. Kern
38, 39 M. Timothy O'Keefe
39 *(both)* M. Timothy O'Keefe
40 Courtesy of The Henry
M. Flagler Museum
41 *(both)* Julie Robinson

OLD SAN JUAN
42, 43 Ken Laffal
44 Ken Laffal
46 *(upper)* Darrell Jones
46 *(lower)* Ken Laffal
47 Roger LaBrucherie/Imagenes Press
48 Roger LaBrucherie/Imagenes Press
49 *(left)* Roger LaBrucherie/Imagenes Press
49 *(right)* Wolfgang Kaehler
50 Roger LaBrucherie/Imagenes Press
51 *(upper)* Wolfgang Kaehler
51 *(lower)* Roger LaBrucherie/Imagenes Press

ST. JOHN
53 Tom Bean
54 *(upper & lower)* Carol Lee
56 Stephen Frink/Waterhouse Stock
Photography
56, 57 Carol Lee
58 *(left)* Carol Lee
58 *(right)* Wolfgang Kaehler
59 Stephen Frink/Waterhouse Stock
Photography
60, 61 Carol Lee
61 *(upper)* Carol Lee
61 *(lower)* Stephen Frink/Waterhouse Stock
Photography
62 Carol Lee
63 *(upper)* Carol Lee
63 *(lower)* Darrell Jones

GALVESTON ISLAND
64 Bob Daemmrich
66 Donne Bryant
68 John Elk
68, 69 John Elk
69 Bob Daemmrich
70 *(upper)* Bob Daemmrich
70 David Muench
71 John Elk
72 Bob Daemmrich
73 *(upper)* John Elk
73 *(lower)* Bob Daemmrich

SANTA CATALINA ISLAND
74, 75 Barrie Rokeach
76 Dave G. Houser
78 Chuck Davis
79 *(left)* Kennan Ward

79 *(right)* Jeff Gnass
80 Jeff Gnass
81 *(upper)* Kennan Ward
81 *(lower)* Jeff Gnass
82 Jeff Gnass
83 *(upper)* Chuck Davis
83 *(lower)* Kennan Ward
84 John Elk
85 *(upper)* Jan Butchofsky
85 *(lower)* Chuck Fishman/Woodfin
Camp & Associates

MONTEREY TO BIG SUR
86, 87 David Muench
88 *(upper)* John Elk
88 *(lower)* Gerd Ludwig/Woodfin
Camp & Associates
90 Al Harvey
90, 91 *(upper right)* Al Harvey
90, 91 *(lower right)* Lynn Radeka
92 *(upper)* Gerry Ellis Nature Photography
92 *(lower)* Rita Ariyoshi
93 David Muench
94 David Muench
94, 95 Timothy Eagan/Woodfin Camp
& Associates
95 Carr Clifton
96 *(upper)* John Elk
96 *(lower)* Bob Miller
97 Bob Miller

THE OLYMPIC PENINSULA
98 Jeff Gnass
100 *(upper left)* Carr Clifton
100 *(lower right)* Art Wolfe
102 *(left)* Alan Briere
102 *(right)* Art Wolfe
103 Wolfgang Kaehler
104 Wolfgang Kaehler
104, 105 Art Wolfe
105 Buddy Mays
106, 107 David Muench
107 Art Wolfe
108 Art Wolfe
109 *(upper right)* Art Wolfe
109 *(lower left)* Dave G. Houser

KAUAI
110, 111 Rita Ariyoshi

112 *(left)* Dave G. Houser
113 *(right)* Jack Jeffrey/Photo Resource
Hawaii Stock
114 *(upper)* Rita Ariyoshi
114 *(lower)* Wolfgang Kaehler
115 *(both)* Rita Ariyoshi
116, 117 Rita Ariyoshi
117 *(upper right)* Jeff Gnass
117 *(lower)* Wolfgang Kaehler
118 Marc Schechter/Photo Resource
Hawaii Stock
119 *(upper)* Jeff Gnass
119 *(lower)* Marc Schechter/Photo
Resource Hawaii Stock

GAZETTEERS
120 Ken Laffal
121 *(both)* Wolfgang Kaehler
122 *(upper right)* Dave G. Houser
122 *(lower left)* Jeff Gnass
123 Carr Clifton
124 Chuck O'Rear/Woodfin Camp
& Associates
125 *(both)* Alan Briere
126 John Elk
127 *(both)* Ken Laffal
128 *(both)* David Muench
129 Tami Dawson/Photo Resource
Hawaii Stock
130 *(both)* Alan Briere
131 Carr Clifton
132 Sylvia Johnson/Woodfin Camp
& Associates
133 *(left)* George Hall/Woodfin Camp
& Associates
133 *(right)* Alan Briere
134 *(both)* Fred Hirschmann
135 Alan Briere
136 Jeff Gnass
137 *(upper)* Dave G. Houser
137 *(lower)* Wolgang Kaehler
138 Cliff H. Smith/f/Stop Pictures
139 *(both)* George H. H. Huey
140 *(both)* Wolfgang Kaehler
141 Wolfgang Kaehler

Back cover photograph by Kennan Ward

ACKNOWLEDGMENTS

Cartography: Map resource base courtesy of the USGS; shaded relief courtesy of the USGS and Michael Stockdale.

The editors would also like to thank the following: Lorraine Doré, Dominique Gagné, and Pascale Hueber.